ANNUAL REPORT

OF THE

Executive Office, Military Department,

OF THE

COMMONWEALTH OF PENNSYLVANIA,

FOR THE

Year ending December 1, 1865.

HARRISBURG:
SINGERLY & MYERS, STATE PRINTERS.
1866.

REPORT.

STATE OF PENNSYLVANIA,
EXECUTIVE OFFICE, MILITARY DEPARTMENT,
Harrisburg, December 1, 1865.

To His Excellency, ANDREW G. CURTIN,
Governor of Pennsylvania:

SIR :—The undersigned have the honor to submit the following report of the operations of this Department, for the year ending December 1, 1865 :

A complete roster of all the officers to whom commissions have been issued during the past year, is herewith attached. It will be seen from it that three thousand three hundred and two commissions were issued during the year. Duplicate commissions, as heretofore, have been issued in great numbers, as applied for.

This roster includes all promotions, as well as original appointments, during the period specified. The promotions incident to your Excellency's order, directing that a rank should be given every meritorious officer and first sergeant, as a brevet for good conduct, when properly recommended, necessarily increased the business of this office very much, for a time, after the close of the war, and as regiments were successively mustered out. That work is now, however, almost closed, and the decrease of the business of the office will render the attendance of more than one **Aid-de-Camp** unnecessary, after the close of a few months, and such Aid can be relieved whenever your Excellency may deem it compatible with the public interest. If, however, your Excellency should continue of opinion, as heretofore intimated, that the work of preparing a military history of the organization of Pennsylvania volunteers and militia, who have been or may be in the "field," as provided for in the thirtieth section of an act approved January 4, 1864, is properly the work of this office, a vast amount of labor yet remains to be done. We have made such preliminary arrangements, with this view, as we deemed best, but in consideration of the insufficiency of the appropriation for the full completion of the work, we have hesitated to go further ; as, to commence such a work, and not carry it through to completion, would be alike unsatisfactory to the people, and the parties having it in charge. The importance to those who have been in the field, and to their surviving relations, as well as to the people at large, of such a work, it is deemed unnecessary here to discuss, your Excellency having already recommended the same to the attention of the Legislature, and they having endorsed its value and importance, by an appropriation for the purpose. The work will be the enduring history of the men who went forward in the armies of the country, from this State, in the great battle of the world, and should be prepared with scrupulous care, and preserved in an enduring form.

The roster of appointments made since the commencement of the war, has, by constant use, become unavoidably much worn and defaced, and should be carefully copied; and the documents connected therewith should be accurately collated, and placed in a condition that will ensure their permanent preservation, and facilitate reference. This work is mainly clerical, and if your Excellency is of opinion that it should be done, requisite appropriations will have to be asked for.

All which is respectfully submitted.

R. BIDDLE ROBERTS,
Colonel and A. D. C.
SAMUEL B. THOMAS,
Colonel and A. D. C.

ERRATUM.

The following appointment, in the Seventy-third Regiment infantry, should be inserted, viz:

Colonel Charles C. Cresson; date of commission, May 20, 1865; rank from May 1, 1865.

ROSTER

OF

COMMISSIONS ISSUED

TO

Officers of Pennsylvania Volunteers,

From December 1, 1864, to December 1, 1865.

WITH DATE OF RANK.

OFFICERS OF THE 111th REGIMENT, PENNSYLVANIA VOLUNTEERS.

Commissioned since December 1, 1864.

RANK.	NAME.	CO. OF RESIDENCE.	DATE OF RANK.	REMARKS.
Lieutenant Colonel.	Benjamin F. Haines....	Luzerne...........	Dec. 13, 1864,	....
Major.................	John B. Overmeyer.....	Lycoming.........	Dec. 13, 1864,	....
Quartermaster.......	Samuel P. Lightcap...	Carbon	June 30, 1865,	....
Company A:				
Second Lieutenant..	Philip W. Kuhns.........	Cumberland.....	June 30, 1865,	....
Company B:				
Captain..............	Harrison Truesdale......	Susquehanna...	May 1, 1865,	....
Do	George W. Bisel.........	Clinton	June 30, 1865,	....
First Lieutenant ...	Robert R. Bittner.......	Do	May 1, 1865,	....
Do	William W. Moore......	Do	June 30, 1865,	....
Second Lieutenant.	George W. Bisel.........	Do	May 1, 1865,	To Captain.
Do	James White	Do	June 30, 1865,	....
Company C:				
Captain..............	Wm. H. M'Laughlin...	Westmoreland...	June 30, 1865,	....
First Lieutenant ...	David P. Bricker.......	Do	June 30, 1865,	....
Second Lieutenant.	John Bodder.............	Do	June 30, 1865,	....
Company D:				
Captain..............	James Moore.............	Lycoming.........	Dec. 13, 1864,	....
First Lieutenant ...	James H. Brown........	Do	Dec. 13, 1864,	....
Second Lieutenant.	James H. Kyle...........	Luzerne...........	May 1, 1865,	....
Do	Charles Harmer.........	Lycoming.........	June 30, 1865,	....

1 MILITARY DEPART.

ELEVENTH REGIMENT—Continued.

RANK.	NAME.	CO. OF RESIDENCE.	DATE OF RANK.	REMARKS.
Company E:				
Captain.............	James J. Briggs.........	Westmoreland...	Dec. 13, 1864,	
First Lieutenant....	Daniel Bonbright.......	Do	Dec. 13, 1864,	
Do	Jacob H. Murdock......	Do	June 30, 1865,	
Second Lieutenant..	Jacob H. Murdock......	Do	May 1, 1865,	To First Lieutenant........
Do	James Thompson........	Do	June 30, 1865,	
Company F:				
Captain.............	Samuel M'Cutchen......	Westmoreland...	June 30, 1865,	
First Lieutenant....	James Cook.............	Do	June 30, 1865,	
Second Lieutenant..	Jeremiah Tawney.......	Do	June 30, 1865,	
Company G:				
Captain.............	Robert Anderson........	Westmoreland...	May 1, 1865,	
First Lieutenant....	John Brenneman........	Do	May 1, 1865,	
Second Lieutenant..	James S. Steele.........	Allegheny........	June 30, 1865,	
Company H:				
First Lieutenant....	Richard W. Morris......	Philadelphia.....	May 1, 1865,	
Do	Nathaniel B. Dilhorn...	Do	June 30, 1865,	
Second Lieutenant..	Richard W. Morris......	Do	Dec. 13, 1864,	To First Lieutenant........
Do	Nathaniel B. Dilhorn...	Do	May 1, 1865,	To First Lieutenant........
Do	Josiah Freese...........	Carbon..........	June 30, 1865,	
Company I:				
Second Lieutenant..	Hiram Delavie..........	Allegheny........	June 30, 1865,	
Company K:				
Second Lieutenant..	Henry B. Temple	Westmoreland...	June 30, 1865,	

OFFICERS OF THE 28th REGIMENT, INFANTRY.

RANK.	NAME.	CO. OF RESIDENCE.	DATE OF RANK.	REMARKS.
Colonel	John Flynn	Philadelphia	Mar. 19, 1864,	
Major	Jacob D. Arner	Carbon	Sept. 30, 1864,	
Adjutant	William S. Witham	Philadelphia	Feb. 8, 1865,	
Company A:				
Second Lieutenant	William Airey	Luzerne	July 21, 1864,	
Company B:				
Captain	William C. Arner		Jan. 18, 1865,	
First Lieutenant	Benjamin F. Mechling		Jan. 18, 1865,	
Second Lieutenant	Charles H. Walker		Jan. 18, 1865,	
Company C:				
Captain	Henry A. Koch	Philadelphia	Sept. 30, 1864,	
First Lieutenant	William S. Witham	Do	Sept. 30, 1864,	To Adjutant
Do	Thomas Munroe	Luzerne	Feb. 8, 1865,	
Second Lieutenant	Albert J. Watt	Cambria	Feb. 8, 1865,	
Company D:				
Second Lieutenant	James Morrison	Philadelphia	June 1, 1865,	
Company E:				
Captain	Simon F. Laurish	Carbon	June 1, 1865,	
First Lieutenant	Douglass M'Lean	Do	June 1, 1865,	
Second Lieutenant	Simon F. Laurish	Do	July 21, 1864,	To Captain
Do	Henry E. Grover	Do	June 1, 1865,	

TWENTY-EIGHTH REGIMENT—Continued.

RANK.	NAME.	CO. OF RESIDENCE.	DATE OF RANK.	REMARKS.
Company F:				
Captain	James F. Knight	Allegheny	Nov. 12, 1864,	
Do	Zachariah Knight	Do	June 30, 1835,	
First Lieutenant	Zachariah Knight	Do	Nov. 12, 1864,	To Captain.
Do	Samuel A. Criste	Cambria	June 30, 1865,	
Second Lieutenant	Samuel A. Criste	Do	Nov. 12, 1864,	To First Lieutenant.
Do	John V. Mortimer	Do	June 30, 1865,	
Company G:				
Captain	Thomas J. Hamilton	Allegheny	Nov. 16, 1864,	
First Lieutenant	James G. Cooper	Do	Nov. 16, 1864,	
Second Lieutenant	William A. M'Gahan	Do	Mar. 30, 1865,	
Company H:				
Second Lieutenant	Henry Hoffer	Allegheny	June 11, 1864,	
Company I:				
Captain	Patrick F. Rourke	Philadelphia	Nov. 29, 1864,	
First Lieutenant	Arnold B. Spink	Cumberland	Nov. 29, 1864,	
Second Lieutenant	Martin J. Rupp	Do	June 1, 1865,	
Company K:				
First Lieutenant	George W. Lees	Philadelphia	May 12, 1865,	
Second Lieutenant	George W. Lees	Do	June 11, 1864,	To First Lieutenant.
Do	James M'Menamin	Do	June 1, 1865,	

EXECUTIVE MILITARY DEPARTMENT. 13

OFFICERS OF THE 29th REGIMENT, INFANTRY.

RANK.	NAME.	CO. OF RESIDENCE.	DATE OF RANK.	REMARKS.
Colonel..................	Samuel M. Zulick........	Philadelphia......	Nov. 3, 1864,	....
Lieutenant Colonel.	George E. Johnson......	.....Do.............	Nov. 3, 1864,	....
Major.....................	Robert P. Dechert.......	.....Do.............	Nov. 3, 1864,	....
Company A :				
Second Lieutenant...	Samuel K. Steever......	Philadelphia......	Feb. 9, 1865,	....
Company C :				
Captain	William Trites...........	Philadelphia......	Feb. 9, 1865,	....
First Lieutenant.....	William F. Stine.........	.....Do.............	July 1, 1861,	To Dec. 18, 1861. Resigned Dec. 18, [1861
Do.........................	Allen J. Metz.............	.....Do.............	Feb. 1, 1865,	....
Company D :				
First Lieutenant.....	Elias T. Cade.............	Philadelphia......	Feb. 9, 1865,	To Captain Company F........
Do.........................	Arthur Gourley..........	.....Do.............	Mar. 15, 1865,	....
Second Lieutenant...	Arthur Gourley..........	.....Do.............	Feb. 9, 1865,	To First Lieutenant............
Do.........................	David M. Black...........	.....Do.............	Mar. 15, 1865,	....
Company F :				
Captain	Elias T. Cade.............	Philadelphia......	Mar. 15, 1865,	....
Second Lieutenant...	Elisha Jones..............	.....Do.............	Mar. 15, 1865,	....
Company G :				
Second Lieutenant...	Harry Shellenberger...	Philadelphia......	Feb. 9, 1865,	....

OFFICERS OF THE 43d REGIMENT, FIRST ARTILLERY—P. R. V. C.

RANK.	NAME.	CO. OF RESIDENCE.	DATE OF RANK.	REMARKS.
Major...............	Theodore Miller..........	Dauphin.........	Jan. 1, 1865,	....
Company A:				
First Lieutenant.....	William R. Brown.......	....	Nov. 26, 1864,	....
Second Lieutenant..	John H. Kline...........	....	Dec. 18, 1864,	....
Company B:				
Captain.............	William M'Clelland.....	Lawrence........	Aug. 8, 1864,	....
First Lieutenant.....	Thomas C. Rice.........	......Do.........	Nov. 22, 1864,	....
Do...........	James A. Gardner.......	......Do.........	Nov. 22, 1864,	....
Second Lieutenant..	James M. Pennypacker,	Chester..........	Nov. 22, 1864,	....
Do...........	John H. Gealy...........	....	Nov. 22, 1864,	....
Company C:				
Captain.............	Sharp L. Richards.......	Luzerne..........	Jan. 11, 1865,	....
First Lieutenant.....	Charles C. Wientz.......	....	Mar. 31, 1865,	....
Second Lieutenant..	Charles C. Wientz.......	....	Feb. 18, 1865,	To First Lieutenant...
Do...........	Frank Langle............	....	Mar. 31, 1865,	....
Company D:				
Captain.............	William Munk............	Lancaster........	Sept. 6, 1864,	....
Company E:				
First Lieutenant.....	William H. Kilgore......	....	Oct. 24, 1864,	....
Do...........	John Perrin..............	....	Mar. 17, 1865,	....
Second Lieutenant..	John Perrin..............	....	Oct. 24, 1864,	To First Lieutenant...
Do...........	John Gnau...............	....	Mar. 17, 1865,	....
Do...........	Joshua E. Price..........	....	June 5, 1865,	....

EXECUTIVE MILITARY DEPARTMENT. 15

Company F:				
Captain	John F. Campbell	Montour	Dec. 21, 1864,	
First Lieutenant	William H. Johnston	Northumberland,	Dec. 21, 1864,	
Second Lieutenant	George W. Mowrer	Montour	Dec. 21, 1864,	
Do	Franklin P. Brockway	Columbia	Dec. 21, 1864,	
Company G:				
Captain	William Jennings		Dec. 21, 1864,	
Do	L. Eugene C. Moore		Mar. 18, 1865,	
First Lieutenant	La Fayette Chandler		Dec. 23, 1864,	Resigned March 8, 1865.
Do	L. Eugene C. Moore		Dec. 21, 1864,	To Captain.
Do	William C. Hays		Mar. 18, 1865,	
Second Lieutenant	L. Eugene C. Moore		Dec. 21, 1864,	To First Lieutenant.
Do	William C. Hays		Dec. 21, 1864,	To First Lieutenant.
Do	William Dixon		Mar. 18, 1865,	
Company H:				
Captain	Lord B. Richards	Luzerne	April 22, 1865,	
First Lieutenant	Horace Templeton		Jan. 11, 1865,	
Second Lieutenant	Samuel L. Richards	Luzerne	Jan. 11, 1865,	
Company I:				
First Lieutenant	Sylvester B. Cameron	Philadelphia	Mar. 20, 1865,	
Do	Lindley J. Taylor	Do	Mar. 20, 1865,	
Second Lieutenant	Wm. D. Schœnlieber	Do	Mar. 20, 1865,	

OFFICERS OF THE 44th REGIMENT, FIRST CAVALRY—P. R. V. C.

RANK.	NAME.	CO. OF RESIDENCE.	DATE OF RANK.	REMARKS.
Company A:				
First Lieutenant...	Joseph F. Moore........	Montgomery......	Nov. 15, 1864,	....
Do............	Samuel Kilpatrick......	Luzerne......	Dec. 26, 1864,	....
Company D:				
Captain..........	Warren L. Holbrook....	....	Oct. 12, 1864,	....
Second Lieutenant.	A. D. Rockey......	....	Oct. 12, 1864,	....
Company F:				
Captain...........	Thomas C. Lebo........	Clinton	Oct. 12, 1864,	....
First Lieutenant...	George W. Fincher......	Berks........	Dec. 26, 1864,	....
Second Lieutenant.	George S. Glisson.......	....Do	Oct. 12, 1854,	To First Lieutenant Company L........
Do............	John Craft...........	Centre.........	Dec. 26, 1864,	....
Company H:				
Captain...........	Vincent Worthington...	Greene........	Dec. 26, 1864,	....
Company L:				
First Lieutenant...	Vincent Worthington...	Greene........	Oct. 12, 1864,	To Captain Company H.......
Do............	George S. Glisson......	Berks........	Dec. 26, 1864,	....
Second Lieutenant.	Joseph Hostetter.......	....	Oct. 12, 1864,	....
Company M:				
Captain...........	A. R. M'Donald.........	Clinton.........	Nov. 11, 1864,	....
First Lieutenant...	A. R. M'Donald.........	....Do	Oct, 12, 1864,	To Captain.......
Do............	Emanuel H. Brittin....	....	Nov. 11, 1864,	....
Second Lieutenant.	John B. Rothenberger.	Berks........	Dec 26, 1864,	....

OFFICERS OF THE 45th REGIMENT, INFANTRY.

RANK.	NAME.	CO. OF RESIDENCE.	DATE OF RANK.	REMARKS.
Chaplain............	F. A. Gast............	Lancaster........	Feb. 17, 1865,	....
Company A:				
Captain............	Roland C. Cheesman...	Centre.............	Dec. 8, 1864,	....
Company B:				
Captain............	John B. Kline.........	Lancaster........	May 1, 1865,	....
First Lieutenant......	Jacob R. Roath........	......Do.........	Mar. 1, 1865,	....
Second Lieutenant...	Moses Mullin.........	......Do.........	Dec. 1, 1864,	....
Company C:				
Captain............	Benj. C. M'Manigel....	Mifflin..........	Sept. 30, 1864,	....
First Lieutenant.....	Adam A. MacDonald...	....Do..........	Jan. 25, 1865,	....
Second Lieutenant...	Michael Hiney........	....Do..........	Jan. 25, 1865,	....
Company D:				
Captain............	Charles Frybarger.....	Centre,...........	Oct. 19, 1864,	....
First Lieutenant.....	William K. Whitlock...	Union.............	Oct. 2, 1864,	....
Second Lieutenant...	Adam A. MacDonald...	Mifflin...........	Jan. 24, 1865,	To First Lieutenant Company C.....
Do............	Joseph L. Hinton......	Centre............	Oct. 2, 1864,	....
Company F:				
Captain............	LaFayette W. Lord....	Delaware, N. Y.,	Dec. 8, 1864,	....
First Lieutenant.....	Jacob Meese..........	Centre............	Jan. 1, 1865,	....
Second Lieutenant..	Jacob Meese..........	...Do............	Jan. 24, 1865,	To First Lieutenant.....
Do............	Wesley Gould.........	Philadelphia.....	May 20, 1865,	....

FORTY-FIFTH REGIMENT—CONTINUED.

RANK.	NAME	CO. OF RESIDENCE.	DATE OF RANK.	REMARKS.
Company G:				
First Lieutenant....	John J. Rogers............	Tioga............	Oct. 19, 1864,	
Second Lieutenant..	Thomas J. Davis..........	Do	Jan. 24, 1865,	
Company H:				
Captain.................	Luke D. Seeley..........	Tioga............	Dec. 1, 1864,	
First Lieutenant....	Hiram Pickering..........	Do	Dec. 1, 1864,	
Second Lieutenant..	Levi R. Robb.............	Do	Jan. 11, 1865,	Killed in action......
Do	Nathan Edwards..........	Do	Apr. 10, 1865,	
Company I:				
Captain.................	Charles M. Hart..........	Tioga............	Jan. 19, 1865,	
First Lieutenant....	James E. Cottin..........	Do	Mar. 1, 1865,	
Second Lieutenant..	Andrew Strong	Bradford	Mar. 1, 1865,	
Company K:				
Captain.................	Edgar Eyde	Lancaster......	Dec. 1, 1864,	
First Lieutenant....	Edgar Eyde...............	Do	Oct. 19, 1864,	To Captain.........
Do	Charles H. Koch.........	Do	Jan. 1, 1865,	
Second Lieutenant..	Charles H. Koch.........	Do	Dec. 1, 1864,	To First Lieutenant...
Do	Ephraim E. Myers.......	Do	Jan. 1, 1865,	

OFFICERS OF THE 46th REGIMENT, INFANTRY.

RANK.	NAME.	CO. OF RESIDENCE.	DATE OF RANK.	REMARKS.
Company A :				
Captain.............	John M. Nolte............	Mifflin.............	Feb. 9, 1865,	....
First Lieutenant....	Enos Rodgers............	...Do.............	Feb. 9, 1865,	....
Second Lieutenant.	James Duncan............	Huntingdon......	July 15, 1865,	....
Company B :				
Captain.............	Elijah Barnes............	Allegheny..........	Feb. 9, 1865,	Honorably discharged June 23, 1865....
Do.......	Jonathan Morgan.........	......Do.............	July 15, 1865,	....
First Lieutenant. ...	William Richards	......Do.............	Feb. 9, 1865,	....
Company C :				
Second Lieutenant.	Owen B. Sigley...........	Northampton	Feb. 9, 1865,	....
Company E :				
Captain.............	Samuel Evans......	Berks............	Feb. 9, 1865,	....
First Lieutenant	William Baron............	....Do.............	Feb. 9, 1865,	....
Second Lieutenant. .	Edmund Cramsie..........	.....Do.............	Feb. 9, 1865,	....
Company F :				
First Lieutenant....	George Beecher..........	Allegheny.........	July 15, 1865,	....
Second Lieutenant. .	Henry Weidensaul......	Dauphin...........	July 15, 1865,	....
Company G :				
First Lieutenant	James H. Cole............	Potter	Sept. 24, 1864,	....
Second Lieutenant. .	Consider E. Lovel........	....Do	July 15, 1865,	....

FORTY-SIXTH REGIMENT—Continued.

RANK.	NAME.	CO. OF RESIDENCE.	DATE OF RANK.	REMARKS.
Company I:				
First Lieutenant.....	Lewis C. Eakman.......	Westmoreland...	July 15, 1865,	....
Company K:				
First Lieutenant.....	Thomas Alderson	Northumberland,	Sept. 23, 1864,	....
Second Lieutenant..	August Shensel..........	....Do	Sept. 23, 1864,	....

OFFICERS OF THE 47th REGIMENT, INFANTRY.

RANK.	NAME.	CO. OF RESIDENCE.	DATE OF RANK.	REMARKS.
Major	George Stroop	Perry	Mar. 30, 1865,	Discharged as Captain June 2, 1865.
Do	Levi Stuber	Lehigh	May 10, 1865,	
Quartermaster	Wm. H. Ginkinger	Do	June 7, 1865,	
Company C:				
First Lieutenant	Christian S. Beard	Northumberland,	May 10, 1865,	
Second Lieutenant	Jacob K. Keeper	Do	May 10, 1865,	
Company D:				
Captain	George Kosier	Perry	Mar. 30, 1865,	
First Lieutenant	George W. Clay	Do	Mar. 30, 1865,	
Second Lieutenant	George W. Clay	Do	Jan. 5, 1865,	To First Lieutenant.
Do	Jesse Meadeth	Do	Mar. 30, 1865,	
Company E:				
Captain	William A. Bachman	Northampton	Jan. 23, 1865,	
First Lieutenant	George A. Diehl	Do	Jan. 23, 1865,	
Second Lieutenant	Frederick J. Scott	Do	Mar. 20, 1865,	Deceased in hands of enemy.
Do	Edward S. Meuner	Do	May 10, 1865,	
Company G:				
Captain	Charles A. Hackman	Lehigh	Nov. 30, 1864,	Discharged as Second Lieut. for disability.
Do	Thomas B. Leisenring	Do	Dec. 17, 1864,	
First Lieutenant	Thomas B. Leisenring	Do	Nov. 30, 1864,	To Captain.
Do	William Steckel	Do	Dec. 17, 1864,	
Second Lieutenant	James M. Krader	Do	Mar. 20, 1865,	

FORTY-SEVENTH REGIMENT—Continued.

RANK.	NAME.	CO. OF RESIDENCE.	DATE OF RANK.	REMARKS.
Company H:				
Captain	Reuben S. Gardner	Perry	Jan. 23, 1865,	
First Lieutenant	James Hahn	Do	Jan. 23, 1865,	
Second Lieutenant	Alfred Billig	Berks	Mar. 20, 1865,	
Company I:				
Captain	Theodore Mink	Lehigh	May 10, 1865,	
First Lieutenant	Allen Lawall	Do	May 10, 1865,	
Second Lieutenant	Wm. H. Haltiman	Do	May 10, 1865,	Died from sun stroke July 24, 1865
Do	Wm. H. Mayers	Do	July 25, 1865,	
Company K:				
Captain	Matthias Miller	Lehigh	Dec. 17, 1864,	
First Lieutenant	Matthias Miller	Do	Nov. 30, 1864,	To Captain
Do	Franklin Beisel	Do	Jan. 1, 1865,	
Second Lieutenant	Elias F. Benner	Do	Jan. 1, 1865,	

OFFICERS OF THE 48th REGIMENT, INFANTRY.

RANK.	NAME.	CO. OF RESIDENCE.	DATE OF RANK.	REMARKS.
Colonel	George W. Gowen	Schuylkill	Jan. 2, 1865,	Killed in action April 2, 1865
Do	Isaac F. Brannon	Do	April 3, 1865,	
Lieutenant Colonel	Isaac F. Brannon	Do	Jan. 2, 1865,	To Colonel
Do	Richard M. Jones	Do	April 3, 1865,	
Major	William H. Hinkle	Do	Jan. 2, 1865,	Mustered out as Captain, March 2, 1865
Do	Richard M. Jones	Do	Mar. 3, 1865,	To Lieutenant Colonel
Do	Jacob Wagner	Do	April 3, 1865,	
Quartermaster	Thomas Bohannan	Do	April 3, 1865,	
Company B:				
Captain	Thomas P. Williams	Schuylkill	Nov. 28, 1864,	
First Lieutenant	George M. Dengler	Do	Mar. 1, 1865,	
Second Lieutenant	John Watkins	Do	Mar. 1, 1865,	
Company C:				
Captain	William Clark	Schuylkill	Oct. 6, 1864,	
First Lieutenant	James Clark	Do	Oct. 6, 1864,	
Second Lieutenant	Henry Weiser	Do	Mar. 1, 1865,	
Company D:				
First Lieutenant	Henry Rothenberger	Berks	Mar. 1, 1865,	
Second Lieutenant	Henry C. Burkhalter	Do	Mar. 1, 1865,	
Company E:				
First Lieutenant	James May	Schuylkill	April 3, 1865,	
Second Lieutenant	John O. M'Elrath	Do	April 3, 1865,	

FORTY-EIGHTH REGIMENT—Continued.

RANK.	NAME.	CO. OF RESIDENCE.	DATE OF RANK.	REMARKS.
Company G;				
Captain	William Auman	Schuylkill	Mar. 3, 1865,	
First Lieutenant	William H. Hardell	Do	Mar. 3, 1865,	
Second Lieutenant	George Farne	Do	Mar. 3, 1865,	
Company H;				
Captain	Alba C. Thompson	Schuylkill	Jan. 2, 1865,	
First Lieutenant	Thomas H. Sillyman	Do	Jan. 2, 1865,	
Second Lieutenant	Peter Radelberger	Do	Mar. 1, 1865,	

EXECUTIVE MILITARY DEPARTMENT.

OFFICERS OF THE 49th REGIMENT, INFANTRY.

RANK.	NAME.	CO. OF RESIDENCE.	DATE OF RANK.	REMARKS.
Colonel	Baynton J. Hickman	Chester	June 29, 1865,	Honorably disch'd at expiration of term.
Do	Amor W. Wakefield	Mifflin	July 14, 1865,	
Lieutenant Colonel	Amor W. Wakefield	Do	June 29, 1864,	To Colonel.
Do	James T. Stuart	Centre	July 14, 1865,	
Major	James T. Stuart	Do	June 29, 1865,	To Lieutenant Colonel.
Adjutant	Robert Davison	Huntingdon	Mar. 1, 1865,	
Chaplain	William Hammond	Philadelphia	Dec. 8, 1864,	
Company A:				
Captain	James M. Wix	Juniata	Jan. 14, 1865,	
First Lieutenant	John B. Rodgers	Mifflin	Jan. 14, 1865,	
Second Lieutenant	William A. Mauger	Juniata	July 14, 1865,	
Company C:				
Captain	James P. Smith	Centre	Dec. 18, 1864,	Hon. disch'd as First Lieut., to take effect
First Lieutenant	Christian Dale	Do	Dec. 18, 1864,	To Capt. Co. H......[May 15, 1865.
Do	John Miller	Do	July 14, 1865,	
Second Lieutenant	James T. Moore	Chester	July 14, 1865,	
Company D:				
Second Lieutenant	Davis H. Lair	Chester	July 14, 1865,	
Company E:				
Captain	Charles S. Whiting	Chester	July 14, 1865,	
First Lieutenant	Lewis K. Pinkerton	Lancaster	Mar. 1, 1865,	Term expired.
Do	George W. M'Cafferty	Chester	July 14, 1865,	
Second Lieutenant	Lewis K. Pinkerton	Lancaster	Oct. 24, 1864,	To First Lieutenant.
Do	John D. Gillespie	Chester	Mar. 1, 1865,	Term expired.
Do	David H. Johns	Juniata	July 14, 1865,	

FORTY-NINTH REGIMENT—Continued.

RANK.	NAME.	CO. OF RESIDENCE.	DATE OF RANK.	REMARKS.
Company F:				
Captain	Joseph H. Downing	Chester	Mar. 1, 1865,	
Second Lieutenant	William H. Glass	Mifflin	Mar. 1, 1865,	
Company G:				
Captain	William M. Irwin	Huntingdon	June 29, 1865,	
First Lieutenant	Hugh T. Johnston	Do	June 29, 1865,	
Second Lieutenant	William Singer	Centre	July 14, 1865,	
Company H:				
Captain	Josiah L. Barton	Juniata	Nov. 1, 1864,	Mustered out as First Lieut. March 12, 1865.
Do	Oliver S. Rumberger	Huntingdon	Mar. 13, 1865,	Term expired.
Do	Christian Dale	Centre	June 27, 1865,	
First Lieutenant	Oliver S. Rumberger	Huntingdon	Nov. 1, 1864,	To Captain
Do	Stephen Trausue	Centre	Mar. 13, 1865,	
Second Lieutenant	Samuel Divin	Huntingdon	July 14, 1865,	
Company I:				
First Lieutenant	David A. Stahl	Snyder	April 7, 1865,	
Second Lieutenant	David A. Stahl	Do	Feb. 26, 1865,	To First Lieutenant
Do	Samuel P. Courtney	Do	July 14, 1865,	
Company K:				
Captain	John F. Reynolds	Allegheny	April 14, 1865,	
First Lieutenant	James H. Bascom	Do	April 14, 1865,	
Second Lieutenant	Thomas M Gillespie	Do	April 14, 1865,	

OFFICERS OF THE 50th REGIMENT, INFANTRY.

RANK.	NAME.	CO. OF RESIDENCE.	DATE OF RANK.	REMARKS.
Colonel	William H. Telford	Bradford	May 1, 1865,	
Lieutenant Colonel	William H. Telford	Do	Feb. 8, 1865,	To Colonel
Do	Samuel K. Schwenk	Schuylkill	May 1, 1865,	
Major	Samuel K. Schwenk	Do	Feb. 8, 1865,	To Lieutenant Colonel
Do	George W. Brumm	Do	May 1, 1865,	
Adjutant	Frank H. Barnhart	Do	Jan. 19, 1865,	
Do	Lewis Crater	Chester	Mar. 20, 1865,	To Captain Company B
Quartermaster	John S. Eckel	Schuylkill	April 1, 1865,	
Chaplain	Hallock Armstrong	Bradford	Jan. 30, 1865,	
Company A:				
Captain	Henry Brodt	Schuylkill	Mar. 2, 1865,	
First Lieutenant	John H. Hening	Do	Mar. 2, 1865,	
Second Lieutenant	William H. Blanchford	Do	Mar. 20, 1865,	
Company B:				
Captain	Frank H. Barnhart	Schuylkill	Mar. 2, 1865,	
First Lieutenant	Alfred J. Stevens	Susquehanna	Jan. 19, 1865,	
Second Lieutenant	Lucien H. Plucker	Berks	Mar. 20, 1865,	
Company C:				
Captain	Charles E. Brown	Schuylkill	Dec. 31, 1864,	
First Lieutenant	John S. Eckel	Do	Dec. 31, 1864,	To Quartermaster
Do	Samuel A. Losch	Do	April 1, 1865,	
Second Lieutenant	Samuel A. Losch	Do	Mar. 2, 1865,	To First Lieutenant
Do	Augustus Mellon	Do	April 1, 1865,	

FIFTIETH REGIMENT—Continued.

NAME.	NAME.	CO. OF RESIDENCE.	DATE OF RANK.	REMARKS.
Company D:				
Second Lieutenant...	Hugh Mitchell........	Susquehanna....	Mar. 20, 1865,	....
Company E:				
Captain................	Richard Herbert......	Lebanon............	Mar. 17, 1865,	Dismissed.............
Do.............	Nicholas H. Sell.......	Berks...............	Aug. 1, 1865,	....
First Lieutenant.....	Nicholas H. Sell.......	...Do...............	Mar. 17, 1865,	To Captain...........
Do.............	Abraham H. De Turk..	...Do...............	Aug. 1, 1865,	....
Second Lieutenant...	Frank H. Forbes.......	Philadelphia......	Mar. 20, 1865,	....
Company F:				
Captain................	Jacob Paulus..........	Allegheny........	May 1, 1865,	....
First Lieutenant.....	Samuel Hess...........	Lancaster.........	May 1, 1865,	....
Second Lieutenant...	Jacob Paulus..........	Allegheny........	Mar. 20, 1865,	To Captain...........
Do.............	Thomas P. Davis......	Schuylkill........	May 1, 1865,	....
Company G:				
Captain................	Charles Forbes........	Bradford..........	May 1, 1865,	....
Second Lieutenant...	Charles Forbes........	...Do...............	Mar. 20, 1865,	To Captain...........
Do.............	John P. Kinney........	...Do...............	May 1, 1865,	....
Company H:				
Captain................	Henry T. Kendall.....	Berks...............	Jan. 19, 1865,	Must. out as Adjutant, expiration of term,
Do.............	John A. Snyder........	...Do...............	Feb. 11, 1865,	............[May 11, 1865.
First Lieutenant.....	Joseph V. Kendall.....	...Do...............	Feb. 11, 1865,	....
Second Lieutenant...	Henry S. Francis......	Chester............	May 1, 1865,	....

Company I:			
Second Lieutenant.	John Denniston	Schuylkill	Sept. 30, 1864,
Company K:			
Second Lieutenant.	George N. Merithew	Bradford	May 1, 1865,

OFFICERS OF THE 51st REGIMENT, INFANTRY.

RANK.	NAME.	CO. OF RESIDENCE.	DATE OF RANK.	REMARKS.
Major..............	Joseph K. Bolton........	Montgomery......	Dec. 18, 1864,	
Adjutant............	Jacob H. Santo..........	Dauphin..........	Nov. 3, 1864,	
Company A:				
Captain............	John H. Colston.........	Montgomery......	Dec. 18, 1864,	
First Lieutenant...	Benjamin P. Thompson...	......Do	Dec. 18, 1864,	
Second Lieutenant.	Edward L. Evans........	......Do	Dec. 18, 1864,	
Company F:				
First Lieutenant...	Francis R. Frey.........	Union............	Dec. 11, 1864,	
Second Lieutenant.	George C. Gutelius......	...Do............	Dec. 11, 1864,	
Company G:				
Captain............	Curtin P. Stoneroad.....	Centre...........	Oct. 20, 1864,	Disch'd for physical disability, Dec. 28, [1864
Do	Thomas D. Reed	....Do...........	Dec. 29, 1864,	
First Lieutenant...	John Gonsallus..........	....Do...........	Dec. 29, 1864,	
Second Lieutenant.	John Gonsallus..........	....Do...........	Oct. 20, 1864,	To First Lieutenant......
Do	George Decker..........		Dec. 29, 1864,	
Company H:				
First Lieutenant...	Hugh M'Clure	Lycoming.........	Mar. 15, 1865,	
Second Lieutenant.	David C. Brewer........	Union............	Mar. 15, 1865,	
Company I:				
First Lieutenant...	Lewis Patterson.........	Montgomery......	Nov. 16, 1864,	
Second Lieutenant.	George W. Patterson....	......Do	Nov. 16, 1864,	

Company K:				
Captain	William S. Mellick	Northampton	Mar. 16, 1865	
First Lieutenant	Jacob Hawk	Do	Mar. 16, 1865	
Second Lieutenant	John Vanlew	Northumberland	Mar. 16, 1865	

OFFICERS OF THE 52d REGIMENT, INFANTRY.

RANK.	NAME.	CO. OF RESIDENCE.	DATE OF RANK.	REMARKS.
Colonel.	John B. Conyngham.	Luzerne.	Mar. 1, 1865,	
Lieutenant Colonel.	John A. Hennessy.	Schuylkill.	Mar. 1, 1865,	
Major.	John A. Hennessy.	Do.	Dec. 6, 1864,	To Lieutenant Colonel.
Do.	George R. Leonard.	Luzerne.	Mar. 1, 1865,	
Quartermaster.	Smith B. Mott.	Do.	Mar. 1, 1865,	
Company A:				
Captain.	John W. Gilchrist.	Luzerne.	Mar. 1, 1865,	
First Lieutenant.	Edward W. Tracy.	Do.	Mar. 1, 1865,	
Second Lieutenant.	Philip G. Killian.	Do.	Mar. 26, 1865,	
Company B:				
Second Lieutenant.	Wm. J. Vaughn.	Wyoming.	June 1, 1865,	
Company C:				
Captain.	Philo M. Burr.	Wyoming.	June 1, 1865,	
First Lieutenant.	William C. Rush.	Clinton.	Mar. 26, 1865,	
Second Lieutenant.	Amos G. Miller.	Philadelphia.	Mar. 26, 1865,	
Company D:				
First Lieutenant.	William Philips.	Union.	May 23, 1865,	
Second Lieutenant.	Edward Zechman.	Do.	May 23, 1865,	
Company E:				
Second Lieutenant.	Alvin Sayles.	Bradford.	Mar. 26, 1865,	

EXECUTIVE MILITARY DEPARTMENT.

Company F:				
First Lieutenant....	Charles E. Britton,......	Luzerne.........	Mar. 26, 1865,	
Second Lieutenant...	George L. Overpeck....	Bradford.........	Mar. 26, 1865,	
Do................	Hiram A. Fuller.........	Luzerne.........	June 4, 1865,	
Company G:				
Captain...............	William Silver...........	Columbia.........	April 22, 1865,	
Do................	Charles R. Kenyon......	Bradford.........	June 1, 1865,	
First Lieutenant.....	William W. Snyder.....	Luzerne.........	Mar. 26, 1865,	
Second Lieutenant...	James W. Evans........	Do.............	Mar. 26, 1865,	
Company H:				
Captain...............	James G. Stevens.......	Luzerne.........	Mar. 26, 1865,	
Do................	Charles C. Battenberg..	Do.............	June 4, 1865,	To Captain.........
First Lieutenant.....	Charles C. Battenberg..	Do.............	Mar. 26, 1865,	
Do................	Joseph R. Roberts	Do.............	June 4, 1865,	To First Lieutenant...
Second Lieutenant...	Joseph R. Roberts.......	Do.............	Mar. 26, 1865,	
Do................	W. W. Archer...........	Do.............	June 4, 1865,	
Company I:				
First Lieutenant.....	Edward W. Smith.......	Luzerne.........	June 8, 1865,	
Second Lieutenant...	Frank Early.............	Do.............	June 8, 1865,	
Company K:				
Captain...............	Henry A. Mott..........	Luzerne.........	Dec. 6, 1864,	
First Lieutenant.....	Thomas Jordan..........	Schuylkill.......	Mar. 26, 1865,	
Second Lieutenant...	Alva Dolph..............	Luzerne.........	June 4, 1865,	

3 MILITARY DEPART.

OFFICERS OF THE 53d REGIMENT, INFANTRY.

RANK.	NAME.	CO. OF RESIDENCE.	DATE OF RANK.	REMARKS.
Chaplain.............	Jos. R. Taylor Gray....	Berks............	Jan. 18, 1865,	....
Company A:				
First Lieutenant....	Tobias B. Schmearer....	Montgomery......	May 15, 1865,	....
Second Lieutenant..	Eli K. Nagle.........	....Do	May 15, 1865,	....
Company B:				
Captain............	Mahlon S. Ludwig.....	Montgomery......	Jan. 4, 1865,	....
First Lieutenant....	Ellet L. Brown	Chester.........	Jan. 4, 1865,	....
Second Lieutenant..	Ellet L. Brown.........	...Do........	Jan. 1, 1865,	To First Lieutenant.
Do	Calvin B. Selheimer....	Mifflin	Jan. 4, 1865,	....
Company C:				
Captain.............	Andrew J. Merritt	Blair............	Mar. 15, 1865,	....
First Lieutenant	John M'Laughlin........	Huntingdon	Oct. 8, 1864,	....
Do.........	Andrew J. Merritt......	Blair............	Mar. 15, 1865,	To Captain........
Do.........	Andrew G. Fleck........	Huntingdon	Mar. 15, 1865,	....
Second Lieutenant..	Andrew J. Merritt......	Blair............	Oct. 8, 1864,	To First Lieutenant.
Do	Daniel Lightner.........	...Do	Mar. 15, 1865,	....
Company D:				
Second Lieutenant..	William H. Kinkead....	Clearfield........	June 1, 1865,	....
Company E:				
Captain.............	Daniel Artman.........	Union...........	May 15, 1865,	....
First Lieutenant ...	Albert H. Hess.........	Indiana.........	June 25, 1865,	....

EXECUTIVE MILITARY DEPARTMENT.

Second Lieutenant..	Albert H. Hess.	Indiana	May 15, 1865,	To First Lieutenant.....
Do	William Ulrich..	Union..	June 25, 1865,	
Company F:				
Captain............	Nathan M. Montange...	Luzerne..	Mar. 16, 1865,	
First Lieutenant....	Lester Race....		Mar. 16, 1865,	
Second Lieutenant..	George W. Thompson..	Wyoming	June 1, 1865,	
Company G:				
First Lieutenant....	Benjamin J. Cushing...	Potter	Jan. 1, 1865,	Disch'd as Second Lieut. March 28, 1865.
Do	George W. Stevens.....	Do	Mar. 29, 1865,	
Second Lieutenant..	George W. Stevens.....	Do	Jan. 1, 1865,	To First Lieutenant....
Do	Asa Toombs............	Do	June 1, 1865,	
Company H:				
First Lieutenant....	Wallace H. Dentler.....	Northumberland,	Oct. 25, 1864,	
Second Lieutenant..	Michael Thornton......	Do	Oct. 25, 1864,	
Company K:				
Captain............	David B. Wineland.....	Westmoreland...	Dec. 22, 1864,	
Second Lieutenant..	Jacob G. Hughes	Do	Dec. 22, 1864,	

OFFICERS OF THE 54th REGIMENT, INFANTRY.

RANK.	NAME.	CO. OF RESIDENCE.	DATE OF RANK.	REMARKS.
Colonel............	Albert P. Moulton......	Berks...........	April 3, 1865,	Hon. dis. as Lt. Col., to date May 30, '65.
Lieutenant Colonel..	Albert P. Moulton......	...Do......	Mar. 20, 1865,	To Colonel..............
Do............	William A. M'Dermitt,	Cambria.........	April 3, 1865,	Hon. dis. as Capt., to date May 30, 1865.
Major...........	Nathan Davis...........	Chester.........	Mar. 20, 1865,	Killed in bat. before Pet., Va., Ap. 2, '65.
Do............	John L. Decker.........	Cambria.........	April 3, 1865,	Honorably discharged as Captain, to take [effect May 15, 1865.
Company A:				
Captain............	John L. Decker.........	Cambria.........	Jan. 1, 1865,	To Major........
Do..........	John M'Cune...........	Indiana.........	April 3, 1865,	Hon dis. as First Lt., to date May 30, '65.
First Lieutenant....	John L. Decker.........	Cambria.........	Dec. 1, 1864,	To Captain.......
Do............	John M'Cune...........	Indiana.........	Jan. 1, 1865,	To Captain.......
Do............	David Bryan...........	Cambria.........	April 3, 1865,	....
Second Lieutenant...	John M'Cune...........	Indiana.........	Dec. 1, 1864,	To First Lieutenant......
Do............	William Stearn.........	Cambria.........	April 3, 1865,	....
Company B:				
First Lieutenant....	John Burgen............	Bucks...........	April 3, 1865,	....
Second Lieutenant...	Andrew C. Nagle.......	Lehigh..........	April 3, 1865,	....
Company C:				
Captain............	Henry Shick............	Northampton....	April 3, 1865,	Honorably discharged as Second Lieu- [tenant, to date May 15, 1865.
First Lieutenant....	George Stineman........	Cambria.........	April 3, 1865,	....
Second Lieutenant...	Levi F. Kipler..........	Montgomery.....	April 3, 1865,	....
Company D:				
Captain............	Robert Smith...........	Berks...........	April 3, 1865,	....

EXECUTIVE MILITARY DEPARTMENT. 37

First Lieutenant...	Edward Cater............	Northampton...	April 3, 1865,	
Second Lieutenant...	Russell P. Abbey.......	Wayne...............	April 3, 1865,	
Company E:				
Captain...............	Charles E. M'Cracken.	Susquehanna.....	April 3, 1865,	
First Lieutenant.....	Charles Felser...........	Philadelphia.....	April 3, 1865,	
Second Lieutenant...	James M. Phillips.	Berks................	May 16, 1865,	
Company F:				
Captain...............	James S. Brown.........	Be...a...............	April 3, 1865,	Honorably discharged as Second Lieu-[tenant, to date May 15, 1865.
First Lieutenant.....	Bartley Cane.............	Cambria............	April 3, 1865,	To First Lieutenant Company B.....
Second Lieutenant...	John Burgen.............	Bucks...............	Sept. 1, 1864,	
Do................	Joseph F. Hummel......	Somerset..........	April 3, 1865,	
Company G:				
Captain...............	William H. Miller......	Northumberland,	April 3, 1865,	
First Lieutenant.....	Samuel Magehan........	Allegheny..........	April 3, 1865,	
Second Lieutenant...	Cyrus Patton.............	Somerset..........	Dec. 1, 1864,	
Do................	George W. Leyberger..	.....Do	April 3, 1865,	
Company H:				
Captain...............	William A. M'Dermitt.	Cambria............	Dec. 1, 1864,	To Lieutenant Colonel...............
Do................	Theodore Way............	Somerset..........	April 3, 1865,	
First Lieutenant.....	Aaron F. Dickey.........	....Do	April 3, 1865,	To Captain Company C ....
Second Lieutenant...	Henry Shick...............	Northampton.....	Dec. 1, 1864,	
Do................	William Eppinger......	Somerset..........	April 3, 1865,	

OFFICERS OF THE 55th REGIMENT, INFANTRY.

RANK.	NAME.	CO. OF RESIDENCE.	DATE OF RANK.	REMARKS.
Colonel	John H. Filler	Bedford	Mar. 25, 1865	
Lieutenant Colonel	John H. Filler	...Do	Dec. 21, 1864	To Colonel
Do	James Metzgar	Cumberland	Mar. 25, 1865	
Major	James Metzgar	...Do	Dec. 21, 1864	To Lieutenant Colonel
Do	George H. Hill	Schuylkill	May 3, 1865	
Quartermaster	James Driscoll	Cambria	Dec. 4, 1864	
Company A:				
Captain	Patrick F. Hodge	Blair	Feb. 15, 1865	
First Lieutenant	John Lynch	Cambria	Feb. 15, 1865	
Second Lieutenant	Celestine M'Mullen	...Do	Feb. 15, 1865	
Company B:				
Captain	Franklin Z. Deppen	Berks	June 1, 1865	
First Lieutenant	Franklin Z. Deppen	...Do	Dec. 24, 1864	To Captain
Do	Elijah B. Smith	...Do	June 1, 1865	
Second Lieutenant	Elijah B. Smith	...Do	Dec. 24, 1864	To First Lieutenant
Do	John H. Kendall	...Do	June 1, 1865	
Company C:				
Captain	Patrick O'Connell	Cambria	Dec. 21, 1864	
Do	James Burke	Dauphin	Mar. 25, 1865	
Do	John Gotshall	...Do	May 10, 1865	
First Lieutenant	Edward Johnson	...Do	Dec. 21, 1864	Honorably discharged
Do	James Burke	...Do	Mar. 21, 1865	To Captain
Do	Samuel Gordon	Cambria	Mar. 25, 1865	

EXECUTIVE MILITARY DEPARTMENT.

Rank	Name	County	Date	Remarks
Second Lieutenant	James Burke	Dauphin	Dec. 21, 1864,	To First Lieutenant
Do	Samuel Gordon	Cambria	Mar. 21, 1865,	To First Lieutenant
Do	George P. Parry	Schuylkill	Mar. 25, 1865,	
Company D:				
Captain	John D. Horn	Bedford	June 12, 1865,	
First Lieutenant	John B. Amos	Do	June 12, 1865,	
Second Lieutenant	Thomas H. Farber	Do	June 12, 1865,	
Company E:				
Captain	William W. Moore	Schuylkill	May 12, 1865,	
First Lieutenant	Daniel Chester	Do	May 12, 1865,	
Second Lieutenant	Daniel Chester	Do	Mar. 21, 1865,	To First Lieutenant
Do	William Challenger	Do	May 12, 1865,	
Company F:				
Captain	Blaney Adair	Indiana	Sept. 29, 1864,	Killed in action
Do	Samuel Moorhead	Do	Mar. 21, 1865,	Killed in action April 2, 1865
Do	Matthew Loughery	Do	May 12, 1865,	
First Lieutenant	John Houston	Do	Sept. 29, 1864,	Honorably discharged
Do	Curtis M'Comish	Do	May 12, 1865,	
Second Lieutenant	Samuel Moorehead	Do	Sept. 29, 1864,	To Captain
Do	Curtis M'Comish	Do	Mar. 21, 1865,	To First Lieutenant
Do	John L. Taylor	Do	May 12, 1865,	
Company G:				
Captain	George H. Miller	Franklin	Mar. 25, 1865,	
First Lieutenant	George H. Miller	Do	Dec. 24, 1864,	To Captain
Do	Daniel Bohannan	Dauphin	Mar. 25, 1865,	
Second Lieutenant	Daniel Bohannan	Do	Dec. 24, 1864,	To First Lieutenant
Do	Henry A. Eisenbise	Mifflin	June 1, 1865,	
Company H:				
Captain	Josiah Hissong	Bedford	Feb. 15, 1865,	

FIFTY-FIFTH REGIMENT—Continued.

RANK.	NAME.	CO. OF RESIDENCE.	DATE OF RANK.	REMARKS.
Captain..........	William A. Dannaker...	Bedford.........	June 7, 1865,	....
First Lieutenant....	Josiah Hissong.........	Do............	Dec. 15, 1864,	To Captain.........
Do	William A. Dannaker...	Do............	Feb. 15, 1865,	To Captain.........
Do	James P. Wogan........	Do............	June 7, 1865,	....
Second Lieutenant.	William A. Dannaker...	Do............	Dec. 15, 1864,	To First Lieutenant...
Do	Daniel A. Hess,........	Do............	Feb. 15, 1865,	....
Do	James P. Wogan........	Do............	May 12, 1865,	To First Lieutenant...
Do	Henry H. Darr.........	Do............	June 7, 1865,	....
Company I:				
Captain..........	Martin V. Sorber.......	Somerset.........	Dec. 15, 1864,	....
First Lieutenant....	Solomon W. Fry........	Blair............	Dec. 15, 1864,	....
Second Lieutenant.	James Brown...........	Philadelphia......	Dec. 15, 1864,	....
Company K:				
Second Lieutenant.	Daniel B. Ritchey......	Bedford.........	Nov. 15, 1864,	....

OFFICERS OF THE 56th REGIMENT, INFANTRY.

RANK.	NAME.	CO. OF RESIDENCE.	DATE OF RANK.	REMARKS.
Colonel	Harry A. Laycock	Luzerne	Mar. 7, 1865,	
Lieutenant Colonel	John T. Jack	Centre	Dec. 26, 1864,	
Do	Harry A. Laycock	Luzerne	Mar. 16, 1865,	To Colonel
Do	John A. Black	Indiana	Mar. 17, 1865,	
Major	Harry A. Laycock	Luzerne	Dec. 26, 1864,	To Lieutenant Colonel
Do	John A. Black	Indiana	Mar. 16, 1865,	To Lieutenant Colonel
Do	George T. Michaels	Centre	Mar. 17, 1865,	
Adjutant	George T. Guier	Union	May 29, 1865,	
Quartermaster	Milton J. Slocum	Wayne	Dec. 26, 1864,	
Chaplain	Benjamin R. Swayne	Do	Sept. 24, 1864,	
Company A:				
Captain	Samuel A. M'Fall	Philadelphia	Dec. 4, 1864,	Discharged—expiration of term
Do	Rufus W. Raymond	Wayne	Mar. 1, 1865,	
First Lieutenant	Benjamin C. Stoddard	Do	May 20, 1865,	
Do	Edson Williams	Susquehanna	April 1, 1865,	
Second Lieutenant	Abner Palmer	Wayne	May 20, 1865,	
Company B:				
Captain	Daniel W. Dougherty	Indiana	Mar. 16, 1865,	
First Lieutenant	Henry O'Niel	Do	Mar. 16, 1865,	
Second Lieutenant	John J. Rankin	Do	Mar. 16, 1865,	
Company D:				
Captain	John H. Kline	Luzerne	Jan. 11, 1865,	
First Lieutenant	John H. Kline	Do	Dec. 26, 1864,	To Captain

FIFTY-SIXTH REGIMENT—Continued.

RANK.	NAME.	CO. OF RESIDENCE.	DATE OF RANK.	REMARKS.
First Lieutenant....	Daniel Clancey......	Philadelphia......	Jan. 11, 1865,	
Second Lieutenant...	Patrick Raid........	......Do..........	Jan. 11, 1865,	
Company F:				
Captain............	John M. Harrish.....	Centre............	Mar. 17, 1865,	
First Lieutenant....	John Limbert........	Union............	Mar. 17, 1865,	
Second Lieutenant...	John Limbert........	......Do..........	Nov. 28, 1864,	To First Lieutenant.
Do...............	John W. Guldin......	......Do..........	Mar. 17, 1865,	
Company G:				
Captain............	James N. Davenport...	Luzerne..........	May 20, 1865,	
First Lieutenant....	Thomas W. Edwards...	......Do..........	May 20, 1865,	
Second Lieutenant...	Edward Phillips......	......Do..........	May 20, 1865,	
Company H:				
Captain............	Samuel H. Bennison...	Clinton...........	Mar. 16, 1865,	
First Lieutenant....	William P. Curwen....	Centre............	Mar. 16, 1865,	
Second Lieutenant...	Frederick Sensor.....	......Do..........	April 30, 1865,	
Company I:				
Captain............	Samuel Healy........	Luzerne..........	Dec. 26, 1864,	Mustered out of service 29th April, 1865.
Do...............	Samuel H. Williams...	Centre............	April 30, 1865,	
First Lieutenant....	Henry C. Cook.......	...Do............	April 30, 1865,	
Second Lieutenant...	Charles Morrow......	....Do...........	April 30, 1865,	
Company K:				
Captain............	Benjamin C. Stoddard.	Wayne'...........	April 1, 1865,	
Do...............	George T. Guier......	Union............	Mar. 20, 1865,	To Adjutant.
First Lieutenant....	Allen M'Call........	Butler............	April 1, 1865,	
Second Lieutenant...	Isaac B. Jones.......	Luzerne..........	April 1, 1865,	

OFFICERS OF THE 57th REGIMENT, INFANTRY.

RANK.	NAME.	CO. OF RESIDENCE.	DATE OF RANK.	REMARKS.
Colonel	George Zinn	Dauphin	Feb. 1, 1865	
Lieutenant Colonel	Lorenzo D. Bumpus	Venango	Nov. 5, 1864	
Do	George W. Perkins	Bradford	Dec. 15, 1864	
Major	Samuel Bryan	Lycoming	Jan. 6, 1865	
Adjutant	Thomas E. Merchant	Philadelphia	April 5, 1865	
Quartermaster	John W. Parke	Mercer	Mar. 1, 1865	
Company A:				
Second Lieutenant	George L. Amey	Susquehanna	Mar. 1, 1865	
Company B:				
Second Lieutenant	William H. Bell	Mercer	April 1, 1865	
Company C:				
Second Lieutenant	George W. Miller	Bradford	Mar. 1, 1865	
Company D:				
First Lieutenant	Cyrus B. Slaven	Crawford	May 19, 1865	
Second Lieutenant	Joseph S. Sharp	Venango	May 19, 1865	
Company E:				
First Lieutenant	John A. Silliman	Crawford	April 18, 1865	
Second Lieutenant	John A. Silliman	Do	Mar. 1, 1865	To First Lieutenant
Do	Joseph Freeman	Do	April 18, 1865	
Company F:				
Captain	Elisha C. Bierce	Mercer	Dec. 2, 1864	

FIFTY-SEVENTH REGIMENT—Continued.

RANK.	NAME.	CO. OF RESIDENCE.	DATE OF RANK.	REMARKS.
Company G :				
Captain...............	Charles W. Forrester...	Columbia........	April 5, 1865,	....
First Lieutenant...	Joseph H. Moore	Blair.....	June 9, 1865,	....
Second Lieutenant..	Pierce Russell............	Bradford.........	June 9, 1865,	....
Company H :				
Captain...............	David Larrish	Sullivan..........	June 9, 1865,	....
First Lieutenant....	William A. Wilson......	Mifflin............	April 7, 1865,	....
Do	William H. H. Hursh..	Cumberland.....	June 9, 1865,	....
Second Lieutenant..	Jacob Weidensall	Blair...............	April 7, 1865,	....
Company I :				
Captain...............	James D. Moore	Mercer............	Nov. 5, 1864,	....
First Lieutenant....	James M. Lewis	Philadelphia....	April 5, 1865,	....
Second Lieutenant..	George W. Lower	Blair...............	April 5, 1865,	....
Company K :				
Second Lieutenant..	Isaac Manes...............	Blair...............	June 9, 1865,	....

OFFICERS OF THE 58th REGIMENT, INFANTRY.

RANK.	NAME.	CO. OF RESIDENCE.	DATE OF RANK.	REMARKS.
Colonel	Cecil Clay	Philadelphia	Nov. 20, 1864,	
Lieutenant Colonel	Robert C. Redmond	Do	Nov. 20, 1864,	
Adjutant	Antony A. Clay	Do	Aug. 2, 1865,	
Quartermaster	Joseph T. Hested	Sullivan	Jan. 31, 1865,	
Company A:				
Captain	William H. Taylor	Philadelphia	Dec. 12, 1864,	
Do	William H. Dexter	Do	May 5, 1865,	
First Lieutenant	William H. Dexter	Do	Jan. 31, 1865,	To Captain.
Do	William Slifer	Chester	May 5, 1865,	
Company C:				
Captain	Henry Robinson	Philadelphia	Jan. 26, 1865,	
First Lieutenant	Joseph M. Hanson, Jr.	Do	Jan. 26, 1865,	
Do	Nathaniel A. M'Keown	Wyoming	Aug. 2, 1865,	
Company D:				
Captain	Newton R. Bunker	Blair	Jan. 31, 1865,	
First Lieutenant	Newton R. Bunker	Do	Dec. 12, 1864,	To Captain.
Do	John Hoffer	Sullivan	Jan. 31, 1865,	
Company E:				
First Lieutenant	Frank W. Davis		Dec. 12, 1864,	
Do	Solomon Pontious		June 14, 1865,	
Company G:				
Captain	Olney V. Cotter	Warren	Dec. 16, 1864,	Dis. as Sec. Lt. Jan. 30, '65, on ex. of term.

FIFTY-EIGHTH REGIMENT—Continued.

RANK.	NAME.	CO. OF RESIDENCE.	DATE OF RANK.	REMARKS.
Captain...............	Thomas Birmingham....	Luzerne............	Jan. 31, 1865,	....
First Lieutenant......	John E. Ault.....	....	Dec. 16, 1864,	....
Company H:				
Captain...............	R. M. Overhiser..........	Cameron...........	April 17, 1865,	....
First Lieutenant.....	R. M. Overhiser...........	...Do.............	Dec. 12, 1864,	To Captain.
Do.....	Marshall J. Hadley......	....	April 17, 1865,	....
Company I:				
First Lieutenant.....	Heber Painter............	Northumberland,	Jan. 31, 1865,	....
Company K:				
First Lieutenant.....	Hans Hanson..............	Potter	Jan. 31, 1865,	....

OFFICERS OF THE 59th REGIMENT, SECOND CAVALRY.

RANK.	NAME.	CO. OF RESIDENCE.	DATE OF RANK.	REMARKS.
Colonel.............	William W. Sanders....	Allegheny.........	Mar. 15, 1865,	
Lieutenant Colonel.	Joseph Steele.............	Armstrong	Mar. 15, 1865,	
Major................	Robert M. Brinton.......	Lancaster.........	Mar. 15, 1865,	
Adjutant............	Samuel Rumford.........	Philadelphia.....	Feb. 23, 1865,	
Company A :				
Captain.............	John T. Prall.............	Philadelphia.....	May 9, 1864,	
First Lieutenant...	John Branigan...........	......Do	Nov. 20, 1864,	
Second Lieutenant..	William Wall.............	Delaware.........	Mar. 3, 1865,	
Company B :				
Captain.............	Charles S. W. Jones.....	Philadelphia.....	Oct. 31, 1864,	
First Lieutenant...	John Thomas Toy.......	Chester...........	Oct. 31, 1864,	
Second Lieutenant..	S. A. Wright.............	Lancaster.........	Oct. 31, 1864,	
Company C :				
Captain.............	Henry G. Dodge.........	Philadelphia.....	Oct. 21, 1864,	Hon. disch'd as Second Lieut. April 25, [1865.
First Lieutenant ...	David R. Maxwell.......	Montgomery.....	Oct. 21, 1864,	
Company D :				
Captain.............	John A. Martin..........	Lancaster.........	Feb. 23, 1865,	
First Lieutenant ...	Henry W. Schultze.....	......Do	Feb. 23, 1865,	
Second Lieutenant..	Henry W. Schultze.....	...... Do	Oct. 16, 1864,	To First Lieutenant.
Do	George G Fraim.........	...... Do	Feb. 23, 1865,	
Company E :				
Captain.............	George W. Schwartz ...	Philadelphia.....	Feb. 23, 1865,	

FIFTY-NINTH REGIMENT—Continued.

RANK.	NAME.	CO. OF RESIDENCE.	DATE OF RANK.	REMARKS.
First Lieutenant....	Francis M. Hafer........	Philadelphia......	Feb. 23, 1865,	....
Second Lieutenant..	Francis M. Hafer........	....Do	Oct. 16, 1864,	To First Lieutenant......
Do	Richard Kelly............	Montgomery......	Feb. 23, 1865,	....
Company F :				
Captain.............	William H. Sheller.....	....	Dec. 8, 1864,	....
First Lieutenant....	Charles S. W. Jones.....	....	Dec. 8, 1864,	....
Do	Horatio L. Snyder	Clearfield..........	Oct. 31, 1864,	....
Second Lieutenant..	Horatio L. Snyder.......	....Do	Oct. 8, 1864,	To First Lieutenant......
Do	Francis H. Armstrong..	Lycoming..........	Oct. 31, 1864,	....
Company G :				
Captain.............	William C. Frew........	Lancaster..........	Feb. 23, 1865,	....
First Lieutenant....	Henry Engle.............	Philadelphia......	Feb. 23, 1865,	....
Company H :				
Captain.............	Aaron K. Seip...........	Northampton.....	Mar. 15, 1865,	....
Company I :				
Second Lieutenant..	Charles W. Foulk.......	Crawford...........	Mar. 3, 1865,	....
Company K :				
Captain.............	Stephen H. Edgett.....	Berks...............	Mar. 3, 1865,	....
First Lieutenant	Stephen H. Edgett.....	....Do	Nov. 26, 1864,	To First Lieutenant......
Do	Jay Hathaway............	Lancaster..........	Mar. 3, 1865,	....
Company L :				

EXECUTIVE MILITARY DEPARTMENT. 49

Captain............	Joseph B. Ferry.........	Tioga............	Feb. 23, 1865,
Second Lieutenant.	Joseph B. Ferry.........	Do............	Oct. 16, 1864,
Do............	William A. Faulkner....	Do............	Mar. 20, 1865,
Company M:			
Second Lieutenant.	James W. Morrow......	....	Oct. 16, 1864,

4 MILITARY DEPART.

OFFICERS OF THE 60th REGIMENT, THIRD CAVALRY.

RANK.	NAME.	CO. OF RESIDENCE.	DATE OF RANK.	REMARKS.
Major................	Charles Treichel........	Philadelphia......	Nov. 21, 1864,	....
Company A:				
First Lieutenant.....	D. M. Kephart..........	Centre............	Jan. 17, 1865,	....
Second Lieutenant...	James T. Ebert.........	....	Nov. 21, 1864,	....
Company B:				
First lieutenant......	Coleman H. Watts......	Cumberland	Jan. 17, 1865,	....
Second Lieutenant...	Calvin D. Ludwig.......	....	Nov. 21, 1864,	....
Company C:				
First Lieutenant.....	Horace W. Hayden.....	Philadelphia.....	Feb. 14, 1865,	....
Company D:				
Captain..............	Alexander B. Frazer....	Philadelphia.....	Jan. 14, 1865,	....
First Lieutenant.....	Alexander B. Frazer....	......Do	Nov. 21, 1864,	To Captain.
Do...................	Andrew Pemberton.....	......Do	Jan. 14, 1865,	....
Company E:				
Captain..............	Thomas Gregg.........	....	Jan. 14, 1865,	....
First Lieutenant.....	Thomas Gregg.........	....	Nov. 21, 1864,	To Captain.
Second Lieutenant...	Samuel M'Kean King....	Philadelphia.....	Nov. 21, 1864,	....
Company F:				
First Lieutenant.....	Frank C. Grugan	Philadelphia......	Nov. 21, 1864,	....
Company I :				

EXECUTIVE MILITARY DEPARTMENT. 51

Captain.............	Thomas Ewing............	....	....	....
First Lieutenant......	Thomas Ewing............	....	Jan. 14, 1862,	To Captain......
Do.................	S. J. M'Farren...........	....	Nov. 21, 1864,	....
Second Lieutenant...	Charles W. Wilson.......	Washington...	Feb. 14, 1865,	....
			Nov. 21, 1864,	
Company M:				
First Lieutenant......	William Wilkeson.......	....	Jan. 17, 1865,	....
Second Lieutenant...	Cornelius O'Donovan...	....	Nov. 21, 1864,	....

OFFICERS OF THE 61st REGIMENT, INFANTRY.

RANK.	NAME.	CO. OF RESIDENCE.	DATE OF RANK.	REMARKS.
Colonel...........	George F. Smith.........	Chester...........	Sept. 29, 1864,	Hon. discharged as of April 26, 1865....
Do...............	Robert L. Orr	Philadelphia.....	Apr. 27, 1865,	
Lieutenant Colonel..	John W. Crosby.........	....Do..............	Feb. 22, 1865,	Killed in action April 2, 1865..........
Do...............	Robert L. Orr............	....Do..............	Apr. 3, 1865,	To Colonel............
Do...............	Charles S. Greene........	....Do..............	Apr. 27, 1865,	
Major.............	Robert L. Orr............	....Do..............	Nov. 30, 1864,	To Lieutenant Colonel......
Do...............	Charles S. Greene........	....Do..............	Apr. 3, 1865,	To Lieutenant Colonel......
Do...............	Oliver A. Parsons........	Luzerne...........	Apr. 27, 1865,	
Adjutant..........	Augustus R. Seiler......	Schuylkill........	Mar. 9, 1865,	
Company A :				
Captain...........	George R. Coleman.....	Philadelphia.....	Dec. 1, 1864,	Disch'd as First Lieut. March 16, 1865.
Do...............	David A. Lukehart......	Indiana............	Mar. 22, 1865,	
First Lieutenant....	David A. Lukehart......	....Do..............	Dec. 20, 1864,	To Captain..........
Do...............	George H. Chanafelt....	Allegheny........	Mar. 22, 1865,	
Second Lieutenant..	George H. Chanafelt....	....Do..............	Dec. 20, 1864,	To First Lieutenant......
Do...............	Joseph H. Clark........	Philadelphia.....	Mar. 22, 1865,	
Company B :				
Captain...........	Caspar Kaufman........	Allegheny........	Dec. 20, 1864,	
First Lieutenant....	Caspar Kaufman........	....Do..............	Nov. 30, 1864,	To Captain..........
Do...............	Robert Kennedy	....Do..............	Dec. 20, 1864,	
Second Lieutenant..	Robert Kennedy	....Do..............	Nov. 30, 1864,	To First Lieutenant......
Do...............	Frederick Calkins.......	....Do..............	Feb. 19, 1865,	
Company C :				
Captain...........	John W. M'Clay........	Allegheny........	Apr. 3, 1865,	

EXECUTIVE MILITARY DEPARTMENT.

First Lieutenant...	John W. M'Clay......	Allegheny......	Nov. 30, 1864,	To Captain............
Do...................	William Gray........	......Do...........	Apr. 3, 1865,	....
Second Lieutenant...	William Gray........	......Do...........	Nov. 30, 1864,	To First Lieutenant...
Do...................	Cyrus Adsil.........	......Do...........	Apr. 3, 1865,	....
Company D:				
Captain..............	Sylvester D. Rhoads...	Luzerne.........	Apr. 27, 1865,	....
First Lieutenant.....	Sylvester D. Rhoads...	......Do.........	Dec. 20, 1864,	To Captain............
Do...................	William Lathrop......	......Do.........	Apr. 27, 1865,	....
Second Lieutenant...	William Lathrop......	......Do.........	Dec. 20, 1864,	To First Lieutenant...
Company E:				
Captain..............	Andrew J. Bingham...	Allegheny......	Jan. 12, 1865,	....
First Lieutenant.....	Andrew J. Bingham...	......Do.........	Nov. 30, 1864,	To Captain............
Do...................	William M. Price.....	......Do.........	Jan. 12, 1865,	....
Second Lieutenant...	William M. Price.....	......Do.........	Nov. 30, 1864,	To First Lieutenant...
Do...................	John M'Vay..........	......Do.........	Jan. 12, 1865,	....
Company F:				
Captain..............	Charles M. Cyphers...	Luzerne.........	Dec. 20, 1864,	....
First Lieutenant.....	Edward R. Robinson...	Philadelphia.....	Dec. 20, 1864,	....
Second Lieutenant...	Augustus R. Seiler....	Schuylkill	Dec. 20, 1864,	....
Do...................	George P. Barnes.....	Luzerne.........	Mar. 9, 1865,	To Adjutant...........
Company G:				
Captain..............	Charles H. Beuley.....	Philadelphia.....	Nov. 30, 1864,	....
First Lieutenant.....	George K. Lutz.......	......Do...........	Nov. 30, 1864,	....
Second Lieutenant...	Abram Davis.........	Indiana..........	Nov. 30, 1864,	....
Company H:				
Captain..............	Horatio K. Tyler......	Allegheny......	Feb. 23, 1865,	....
First Lieutenant.....	Samuel B. M'Kowen...	......Do...........	Feb. 23, 1865,	....
Second Lieutenant...	William H. H. Tyler..	......Do...........	Feb. 23, 1865,	....

SIXTY-FIRST REGIMENT—Continued.

RANK.	NAME.	CO. OF RESIDENCE.	DATE OF RANK.	REMARKS.
Company I:				
Captain............	Isaac Wright............	Allegheny............	Feb. 23, 1865,	....
First Lieutenant...	William Graham.........	Do	Feb. 23, 1865,	....
Second Lieutenant..	Frank Bowen............	Do	Feb. 23, 1865,	....
Do	John W. Calvert.........	Do	June 7, 1865,	....
Company K:				
Captain............	Henry C. Scriver........	Allegheny............	Mar. 24, 1865,	....
First Lieutenant...	Jeremiah R. Murphy.....	Do	Mar. 24, 1865,	....
Second Lieutenant..	Charles Weaver..........	Do	Mar. 24, 1865,	....

OFFICERS OF THE 64th REGIMENT, FOURTH CAVALRY.

RANK.	NAME.	CO. OF RESIDENCE.	DATE OF RANK.	REMARKS.
Major...........	William B. Mays........	Venango.........	Oct. 21, 1864,	Killed April 7, 1865...
Do.............	Duncan C. Phillips.....	Allegheny.......	Jan. 1, 1865,	Resigned.............
Do.............	Robert J. Phipps.......	Venango.........	Feb. 17, 1865,	Honorably discharged May 17, 1865..
Do.............	Napoleon J. Horrell....	Westmoreland....	April 8, 1865,	
Do.............	John C. Paul...........	......Do.........	May 18, 1865,	
Adjutant........	William B. M'Elroy.....	......Do.........	May 23, 1865,	
Quartermaster..	Lewis Young............	Allegheny.......	Jan. 2, 1865,	
Company A:				
Captain.........	William Hyndman........		Feb. 22, 1865,	
First Lieutenant.	William Hyndman........		Oct. 21, 1864,	To Captain...........
Do.............	Robert T. Atwell.......		Feb. 22, 1865,	
Second Lieutenant..	George W. Moss.........		Dec. 13, 1864,	To Captain Company F....
Do.............	George W. Mickle.......		Feb. 22, 1865,	
Company B:				
Captain.........	James H. Grenet........		Feb. 22, 1865,	
First Lieutenant.	James H. Grenet........		Nov. 15, 1864,	To Captain...........
Do.............	William K. Sinclair....		Feb. 22, 1865,	
Second Lieutenant..	William K. Sinclair....		Nov. 15, 1864,	To First Lieutenant....
Do.............	Samuel Groves..........		Feb. 22, 1865,	
Company C:				
Captain.........	Wilson Waigle..........	Westmoreland....	July 1, 1865,	
First Lieutenant.	Wilson Waigle..........	......Do.........	Nov. 15, 1864,	To Captain...........
Do.............	Tobias Rosenster.......	......Do.........	July 1, 1865,	
Second Lieutenant..	Tobias Rosenster.......	......Do.........	Nov. 15, 1864,	To First Lieutenant....

SIXTY-FOURTH REGIMENT—Continued.

RANK.	NAME.	CO. OF RESIDENCE.	DATE OF RANK.	REMARKS.
Second Lieutenant...	William Thompson......	Westmoreland...	July 1, 1865,	
Company D:				
Captain.............	John M. Coulter........	Westmoreland ..	May 18, 1865,	To Captain.......
First Lieutenant...	John M. Coulter........	......Do........	Nov. 15, 1864,	
Do.........	Albert W. Martin.......	......Do........	May 18, 1865,	To First Lieutenant.
Second Lieutenant...	Albert W. Martin.......	......Do........	Feb. 22, 1865,	
Do.........	William H. Shick.......	......Do........	May 18, 1865,	To First Lieutenant.
Company E:				
Captain.............	William K. Gillespie....	Allegheny......	Feb. 22, 1865,	
First Lieutenant...	Thomas L. Stewart.....	......Do........	April 20, 1865,	
Company F:				
Captain.............	George W. Moss........	Allegheny......	Feb. 22, 1865,	
First Lieutenant...	Hiram N. Dubbs........	......Do........	Mar. 15, 1865,	To First Lieutenant.
Second Lieutenant...	Hiram N. Dubbs........	......Do........	Oct. 22, 1864,	
Do.........	Adam M'Knight........	......Do........	Mar. 15, 1865,	
Company G:				
Captain.............	Daniel C. Boggs........	Allegheny......	Oct. 21, 1864,	To Captain Company I.
First Lieutenant...	Andrew Nellis..........	......Do........	Oct. 21, 1864,	
Do.........	Alexander Matchet.....	......Do........	April 22, 1865,	Discharged March 25, 1865...
Second Lieutenant...	Richard Whittaker.....	......Do........	Oct. 21, 1864,	
Company H:				
Captain.............	George W. Wilson......	Venango........	Mar. 20, 1865,	

EXECUTIVE MILITARY DEPARTMENT. 57

First Lieutenant.....	Josiah J. Watkins.......	Venango..........	Dec. 2, 1864,	Discharged March 25, 1865......
Do................	Adelbert M. Beaty.......	Do............	April 20, 1865,	
Second Lieutenant...	David P. Lamb...........	Do............	April 20, 1865,	
Company I:				
Captain..............	Andrew Nellis...........	Allegheny......	Feb. 22, 1865,	
First Lieutenant.....	John B. Hoge............	Mercer..........	Oct. 18, 1864,	
Second Lieutenant...	Albert J. Serry.........		Oct. 18, 1864,	
Company K:				
Captain..............	James R. Grant..........	Venango..........	Oct. 19, 1864,	
First Lieutenant.....	George W. Wise..........	Do............	Oct. 19, 1864,	To First Lieutenant Company A........
Second Lieutenant...	Robert T. Atwell........		Oct. 19, 1864,	Died April 12, 1865, from wounds re-
Do................	John A. Welton..........		Feb. 22, 1865,	[ceived in battle.
Do................	J. W. Russell...........		April 13, 1865,	
Company L:				
Captain..............	John P. Barr............	Venango..........	Oct. 21, 1864,	
First Lieutenant.....	Henry S. Bickel.........		Oct. 21, 1864,	
Second Lieutenant...	George W. Wilson........	Venango..........	Oct. 21, 1864,	To Captain Company H...............
Do................	Abner J. Pryer..........	Do............	Mar. 20, 1865,	
Company M:				
Captain..............	John C. Harper..........		Nov. 15, 1864,	Discharged.....
Do................	Samuel B. N. King.......		Feb. 22, 1865,	To Captain..............
First Lieutenant.....	Samuel B. N. King.......		Nov. 15, 1864,	Killed March 31, 1865..........
Do................	Charles E. Nugent.......		Feb. 22, 1865,	
Do................	Peter Burke.............		April 1, 1865,	
Second Lieutenant...	Peter Burke.............		Feb. 22, 1865,	To First Lieutenant......

OFFICERS OF THE 65th REGIMENT, FIFTH CAVALRY

RANK.	NAME.	CO. OF RESIDENCE.	DATE OF RANK.	REMARKS.
Major	Justinian Alman	Philadelphia	Apr. 1, 1865	
Do	H. W. Paul	Do	Apr. 26, 1865	
Adjutant	J. Edwards Bayley	Bucks	Feb. 23, 1865	Hon. discharged, to date May 15, 1865
Do	E. M'Mahon		July 8, 1865	
Quartermaster	Samuel M. King	Philadelphia	June 23, 1865	
Company B:				
Captain	William E. A. Bird	Philadelphia	Dec. 3, 1864	Discharged
Do	Jacob Wolf	Do	Feb. 23, 1865	
First Lieutenant	Jacob Wolf	Do	Dec. 3, 1864	To Captain
Do	Henry P. Robinson	Do	Feb. 23, 1865	
Second Lieutenant	Henry P. Robinson	Do	Dec. 3, 1864	To First Lieutenant
Do	Frank Kleing	Do	Feb. 23, 1865	
Company C:				
First Lieutenant	Gustav Reinecker	Philadelphia	Dec. 3, 1864	To Captain Company E
Do	Aaron W. Snyder	Montgomery	Apr. 26, 1865	
Second Lieutenant	Aaron W. Snyder	Do	Dec. 3, 1864	To First Lieutenant
Do	John W. Blake	Philadelphia	Apr. 26, 1865	
Company D:				
Captain	George Smith	Philadelphia	Apr. 26, 1865	
First Lieutenant	Thomas F. Roberts	Montgomery	Dec. 3, 1864	
Second Lieutenant	Joshua E. Dyer	Delaware	Dec. 3, 1864	Deceased
Do	John Harding	Lycoming	Apr. 26, 1865	
Company E:				

EXECUTIVE MILITARY DEPARTMENT.

Captain................	Gustav Reinecker.......	Philadelphia.....	Apr. 26, 1865,	
First Lieutenant......	August Shroeder........	...Do	Dec. 3, 1864,	
Second Lieutenant...	William Vogel..........	...Do	Dec. 3, 1864,	
Company H :				
Captain................	Henry A. Vezin.........	Philadelphia.....	Dec. 22, 1864,	
Second Lieutenant...	Jacob E. Bayley	......Do	Dec. 3, 1864,	Hon. discharged, to date May 15, 1865.
Do.....................	John C. Gauler	......Do	Feb. 23, 1865,	
Company I :				
First Lieutenant......	Patrick B. Stokes	Philadelphia.....	Dec. 3, 1864,	
Second Lieutenant...	Thomas Fitzpatrick.....	......Do	Dec. 3, 1864,	
Company K :				
Captain................	William H. Shaeffer....	Lycoming	Feb. 23, 1865,	
First Lieutenant......	Josiah Anderson........	......Do	Feb. 23, 1865,	
Second Lieutenant...	James H. Tilburg.......	......Do	Feb. 23, 1865,	
Company L :				
Captain................	John Cook Brown.......	Philadelphia.....	Feb. 23, 1865,	
First Lieutenant......	Henry Forth............	Allegheny........	Feb. 23, 1865,	
Second Lieutenant...	M. V. Smith............	......Do	Feb. 23, 1865,	

OFFICERS OF THE 67th REGIMENT, INFANTRY.

RANK.	NAME.	CO. OF RESIDENCE.	DATE OF RANK.	REMARKS.
Colonel	Harry White	Indiana	Jan. 18, 1865	
Do	John C. Carpenter	Do	June 1, 1865	
Lieutenant Colonel	Harry White	Do	Oct. 31, 1864	To Colonel
Do	John C. Carpenter	Do	May 15, 1865	To Colonel
Do	Peter Marsh	Monroe	June 14, 1865	
Major	John F. Young	Indiana	Oct. 31, 1864	Mustered out of service; term expired.
Do	John C. Carpenter	Do	May 1, 1865	To Lieutenant Colonel
Do	Samuel M'Henry	Do	June 14, 1865	
Adjutant	Daniel W. Brower	Chester	Dec. 13, 1864	
Quartermaster	Samuel Flint	Westmoreland	May 1, 1865	
Company B:				
Captain	Samuel M'Henry	Indiana	Apr. 18, 1865	To Major
Do	Nathaniel Z. Seitz	York	June 14, 1865	
First Lieutenant	Nathaniel Z. Seitz	Do	Apr. 18, 1865	To Captain
Do	Dallas Sutton	Venango	June 14, 1865	
Second Lieutenant	Dallas Sutton	Do	Apr. 18, 1865	To First Lieutenant
Do	John Kinter	Indiana	June 14, 1865	
Company C:				
Captain	Horace O. Thayer	Wayne	Apr. 1, 1865	
Do	Hiram T. Starke	Do	June 14, 1865	
First Lieutenant	Hiram T. Starke	Do	Feb. 2, 1865	To Captain
Do	Horace P. Warfield	Do	June 14, 1865	
Second Lieutenant	Horace P. Warfield	Do	Apr. 1, 1865	To First Lieutenant
Do	Moses P. Vanawken	Pike	June 14, 1865	

EXECUTIVE MILITARY DEPARTMENT. 61

Company D:				
Captain............	Francis A. Hubbell....	Wayne.....	May 1, 1865,	....
First Lieutenant...	William H. Altemus...	Monroe	Feb. 14, 1865,	....
Second Lieutenant...	Franklin Stout.........	....Do	Apr. 1, 1865,	....
Company E:				
Captain............	J. C. Hagenbach......	Northampton...	Apr. 18, 1865,	....
First Lieutenant...	William A. Roger......	Indiana	Apr. 1, 1865,	....
Second Lieutenant...	William Kellar........	....Do	May 1, 1865,	....
Company F:				
Captain............	Martin Flick...........	Clarion...........	Apr. 1, 1865,	....
First Lieutenant...	G. W. Sloan...........	Indiana	May 1, 1865,	....
Company G:				
Captain............	Thomas Madden.......	Monroe...........	June 14, 1865,	....
First Lieutenant...	Thomas Madden.......	Wayne............	Apr. 1, 1865,	To Captain........
Do............	Jacob Andrews	Monroe..........	June 14, 1865,	....
Second Lieutenant...	Thomas Madden.......	Wayne............	Feb. 2, 1865,	To First Lieutenant...
Do............	Jacob Andrews.........	Monroe...........	Apr. 1, 1865,	To First Lieutenant.
Company H:				
Captain............	George W. Griffin.......	Northampton....	Apr. 1, 1865,	....
First Lieutenant...	John Larimer..........	Westmoreland ...	May 1, 1865,	....
Second Lieutenant...	Thomas Fagan.........	Philadelphia.....	June 14, 1865,	....
Company I:				
Captain............	John F. M'Donald......	Allegheny........	Apr. 18, 1865,	....
First Lieutenant...	Frank P. Rohen........	....Do............	Apr. 18, 1865,	....
Second Lieutenant...	John Dyer, Jr..........	....Do............	Apr. 18, 1865,	....
Company K:				
Captain............	Asaph M. Clark........	Jefferson........	May 1, 1865,	....
First Lieutenant...	Asaph M. Clark........	....Do..........	Dec. 13, 1864,	To Captain........
Do............	Samuel Shoener........	Schuylkill.......	June 14, 1865,	....

OFFICERS OF THE 68th REGIMENT, INFANTRY.

RANK.	NAME.	CO. OF RESIDENCE.	DATE OF RANK.	REMARKS
Major............	Michael Fulmer.........	Philadelphia......	April 3, 1865,	....
Company A:				
Captain............	Charles H. Miller........	....	Feb. 7, 1865,	....
First Lieutenant......	John S. Sorver.........	Philadelphia......	Feb. 7, 1865,	....
Company C:				
Captain............	John Devlin.........	Philadelphia......	April 19, 1865,	....
First Lieutenant......	Hiram M'Allister......	......Do.	June 1, 1865,	....
Company H:				
Second Lieutenant...	Samuel D. Neiman.......	Philadelphia......	June 1, 1865,	....
Company K:				
First Lieutenant......	William Gregory.........	Philadelphia......	Feb. 7, 1865,	....

OFFICERS OF THE 69th REGIMENT, INFANTRY.

RANK.	NAME.	CO. OF RESIDENCE.	DATE OF RANK.	REMARKS.
Colonel	William Davis	Philadelphia	Jan. 1, 1865	
Lieutenant Colonel	James O'Reilly	Do	June 16, 1865	
Major	James O'Reilly	Do	Mar. 1, 1865	To Lieutenant Colonel.
Do	John M'Hugh	Do	June 16, 1865	
Quartermaster	Draper C. Smith	Do	Nov. 26, 1864	
Company A:				
First Lieutenant	Patrick Moran	Philadelphia	June 16, 1865	
Second Lieutenant	Thomas Gunning	Do	June 16, 1865	
Company C:				
Captain	John Conner	Philadelphia	Mar. 1, 1865	
First Lieutenant	Connell M'Glinchy	Do	June 16, 1865	
Second Lieutenant	Michael Brady	Do	June 16, 1865	
Company D:				
Captain	Michael Fay	Philadelphia	Mar. 1, 1865	
First Lieutenant	James Gallagher	Do	June 16, 1865	
Second Lieutenant	Patrick J. Connolly	Do	June 16, 1865	
Company E:				
First Lieutenant	Joseph M'Garvey	Philadelphia	June 16, 1865	
Company F:				
Captain	James Welsh	Philadelphia	June 16, 1865	
First Lieutenant	Michael Trainer	Do	June 16, 1865	
Second Lieutenant	Thomas Stackhouse	Do	June 16, 1865	

SIXTY-NINTH REGIMENT—Continued.

RANK.	NAME.	CO. OF RESIDENCE.	DATE OF RANK.	REMARKS.
Company G:				
First Lieutenant...	James Branken...........	Philadelphia......	June 16, 1865,	
Second Lieutenant...	Thomas Stinson..........	......Do............	June 16, 1865,	
Company H:				
Captain...............	Dennis Loughery........	Philadelphia......	Nov. 1, 1864,	
First Lieutenant.....	Charles B. Tanner......	......Do............	Nov. 1, 1864,	
Do...................	Henry Convey...........	......Do............	June 16, 1865,	Resigned May 25, 1865.
Second Lieutenant...	James Barr...............	......Do............	June 16, 1865,	
Company I:				
Captain...............	Joseph W. Garrett......	Philadelphia......	Feb. 17, 1865,	
First Lieutenant.....	George P. Deichler.....	Lancaster.........	Feb. 17, 1865,	
Company K:				
Captain...............	Theodore F. Stratton...	Philadelphia......	May 13, 1864,	
First Lieutenant.....	William H. Haskins.....	......Do............	June 16, 1865,	
Second Lieutenant...	Hugh Flooney	......Do............	June 16, 1865,	

OFFICERS OF THE 70th REGIMENT, SIXTH CAVALRY.

RANK.	NAME.	CO. OF RESIDENCE.	DATE OF RANK.	REMARKS.
Colonel	Charles L. Leiper	Delaware	Mar. 20, 1865,	
Lieutenant Colonel	Charles G. Leiper	Do	Jan. 2, 1865,	To Colonel.
Do	Albert P. Morrow	Philadelphia	Mar. 20, 1865,	
Major	Albert P. Morrow	Do	Jan. 2, 1865,	To Lieutenant Colonel.
Do	Abram D. Price	Do	Mar. 20, 1865,	
Do	Charles B. Coxe	Do	Mar. 20, 1865,	
Do	Bernard H. Harkness	Do	Mar. 20, 1865,	
Adjutant	Wm. Redwood Wright	Do	Mar. 20, 1865,	To Captain Company B.
Do	C. A. Newhall	Do	Mar. 21, 1865,	
Quartermaster	J. W. Milhenny	Do	Mar. 20, 1865,	To Captain Company G.
Commissary	Edward Whiteford	Do	Dec. 6, 1864,	
Do	Charles White	Do	Feb. 7, 1865,	
Company A:				
Captain	T. Campbell Oakman	Philadelphia	Mar. 21, 1865,	
First Lieutenant	Michael Golden	Do	May 7, 1865,	
Company B:				
Captain	Wm. Redwood Wright	Philadelphia	Mar. 21, 1865,	
First Lieutenant	G. W. Buckingham	Do	May 7, 1865,	
Company C:				
Captain	Isaac T. Moffat	Philadelphia	Mar. 20, 1865,	
First Lieutenant	William Scott	Do	May 7, 1865,	
Company D:				
Captain	C. A. Vernon	Philadelphia	Mar. 20, 1865,	

5 MILITARY DEPART.

SEVENTIETH REGIMENT—Continued.

RANK.	NAME.	CO. OF RESIDENCE.	DATE OF RANK.	REMARKS.
First Lieutenant....	John Laird.............	Philadelphia.....	June 9, 1865,	....
Second Lieutenant...	James Magee..........	Do	Mar. 20, 1865,	....
Do...........	E. B. Green............	Do	May 7, 1865,	....
Company E:				
Captain.............	Samuel R. Colladay....	Philadelphia.....	Mar. 20, 1865,	....
First Lieutenant....	Abiah T. Smedley......	Chester........	June 9, 1865,	....
Second Lieutenant...	Humphrey S. Arnold...	Delaware........	May 7, 1865,	....
Company F:				
Captain.............	Andrew L. Lanigan....	Philadelphia.....	Mar. 20, 1865,	....
First Lieutenant....	Joseph D. Price.......	Do	Mar. 20, 1865,	....
Company G:				
Captain.............	Edward Whiteford.....	Philadelphia....	Jan. 2, 1865,	....
First Lieutenant....	C. A. Vernon..........	Do	Feb. 7, 1865,	To Captain Company D.......
Do...........	T. Campbell Oakman...	Do	Mar. 20, 1865,	To Captain Company A.......
Second Lieutenant...	T. Campbell Oakman...	Do	Mar. 4, 1865,	To First Lieutenant........
Do...........	John Laird............	Do	May 7, 1865,	To First Lieutenant Company D......
Company H:				
Captain.............	Bernard H. Harkness...	Philadelphia	Dec. 6, 1864,	To Major................
Do...........	James Henry Workman,	Do	Mar. 20, 1865,	....
First Lieutenant....	Wilmer H. Foard.......	Do	Dec. 6, 1864,	....
Do...........	Samuel R. Colladay....	Do	Feb. 7, 1865,	To Captain Company E.......
Do...........	John M. Odenheimer...	Do	Mar. 20, 1865,	....
Do...........	Daniel B. Hertz........	Do	May 7, 1865,	....

EXECUTIVE MILITARY DEPARTMENT.

Second Lieutenant.	J. W. M'Ilhenney	Philadelphia	Dec. 6, 1864,	To Quartermaster
Do	Daniel B. Hertz	Do	Mar. 20, 1865,	To First Lieutenant
Company I:				
Captain	Edward J. Hazel	Philadelphia	May 7, 1865,	
First Lieutenant	John K. Marshal	Adams	Feb. 16, 1865,	
Second Lieutenant	Joseph D. Price	Philadelphia	Dec. 6, 1864,	To First Lieutenant Company F
Do	J. W. Buckingham	Do	Mar. 20, 1865,	To First Lieutenant Company B
Company K:				
Captain	Archer Maris	Philadelphia	Jan. 2, 1865,	
First Lieutenant	J. Henry Tondy	Do	Mar. 20, 1865,	
Second Lieutenant	J. Henry Tondy	Do	Dec. 6, 1864,	To First Lieutenant
Company L:				
Captain	Levis Miller, Jr.	Delaware	Mar. 20, 1865,	
Second Lieutenant	Wm. Redwood Wright	Philadelphia	Dec. 6, 1864,	To Adjutant
Do	William Scott	Do	Mar. 20, 1865,	
Company M:				
Captain	R. M. Sheppard	Philadelphia	Feb. 7, 1865,	
First Lieutenant	William Carey	Do	May 7, 1865,	
Second Lieutenant	John M. Odenheimer	Do	Dec. 6, 1864,	To First Lieutenant Company H
Do	William Carey	Do	Mar. 20, 1865,	To First Lieutenant

OFFICERS OF THE 73d REGIMENT, INFANTRY.

RANK.	NAME.	CO. OF RESIDENCE.	DATE OF RANK.	REMARKS.
Major...............	Christian H. Goebel....	Philadelphia.....	Aug. 21, 1864,	
Adjutant.............	Seth Slocum	......Do	May 1, 1865,	
Company A:				
First Lieutenant....	James Kinney...........	Philadelphia.....	Feb. 14, 1865,	
Second Lieutenant..	Theodore Myers.........	......Do	Feb. 14, 1865,	
Company B:				
First Lieutenant....	Frederick Martin	Philadelphia.....	May 1, 1865,	
Second Lieutenant..	Edward Buell	......Do	May 1, 1865,	To First Lieutenant Company H.....
Company C:				
First Lieutenant....	Peter Carbrey...........	Philadelphia.....	June 1, 1865,	
Company D:				
Captain	John Goebel	Philadelphia.....	May 1, 1865,	
First Lieutenant....	John Steel...............	......Do	May 1, 1865,	
Do	Peter Rhein.............	......Do	June 1, 1865,	
Company E:				
Captain	William Ker	Philadelphia.....	Nov. 6, 1864,	
Do.................	Edwin Belcher..........	......Do	May 1, 1865,	
First Lieutenant....	William Dennell.........	......Do	May 1, 1865,	
Company F:				
Captain	Charles Moyer	Philadelphia.....	May 1, 1865,	
First Lieutenant....	Henry Myer.............	......Do	May 1, 1865,	

Company G:			
Captain	Adam C. Dieffenbach	Philadelphia	May 1, 1865,
Company H:			
Captain	Alexander Harlfinger	Philadelphia	May 1, 1865,
First Lieutenant	Edward Buell	Do	June 1, 1865,
Second Lieutenant	Earnest H. Diver	Do	May 1, 1865,
Company I:			
Captain	George Wild	Philadelphia	July 6, 1864,
First Lieutenant	Henry Miller	Do	Feb 14, 1865,
Company K:			
Captain	John M'Govern	Philadelphia	Feb. 14, 1865,
Do	Jacob I.bner	Do	May 1, 1865,
First Lieutenant	James Gallagher	Do	June 1, 1865,

OFFICERS OF THE 74th REGIMENT, INFANTRY.

RANK.	NAME.	CO. OF RESIDENCE.	DATE OF RANK.	REMARKS.
Colonel	Gotleib Hoburg	Philadelphia	April 1, 1865,	
Lieutenant Colonel	Carl Veitenheimer	Do	April 1, 1865,	
Major	Elias P. Rohbach	Northumberland	April 1, 1865,	
Adjutant	John H. Louis	Philadelphia	April 1, 1865,	
Do	Robert Bertram	Do	May 2, 1865,	
Quartermaster	Everhart Gertz	Do	April 1, 1865,	
Company A:				
Captain	Samuel J. Pealer	Columbia	Mar. 12, 1865,	Discharged May 8, 1865
Do	John W. Beishline	Do	June 1, 1865,	To Captain
First Lieutenant	John W. Beishline	Do	Mar. 12, 1865,	
Do	John F. Miller	Wyoming	June 1, 1865,	
Second Lieutenant	John F. Miller	Do	Mar. 12, 1865,	To First Lieutenant
Company B:				
Captain	John G. Wilson	Indiana	Mar. 11, 1865,	Discharged May 8, 1865
Do	Peter C. Spencer	Do	May 9, 1865,	
First Lieutenant	Peter C. Spencer	Do	Mar. 13, 1865,	To Captain
Second Lieutenant	Perry E. Horne	Union	Mar. 13, 1865,	
Company C:				
Captain	Elias P. Rohbach	Union	Mar. 29, 1865,	To Major
Do	John H. Lewis	Snyder	May 2, 1865,	
First Lieutenant	Samuel S. Hendricks	Northumberland	Mar. 29, 1865,	Discharged May 12, 1865
Second Lieutenant	Clinton D. Rohbach	Do	Mar. 29, 1865,	Discharged May 31, 1865
Do	Benjamin F. Bright	Do	May 2, 1865,	

EXECUTIVE MILITARY DEPARTMENT. 71

Company D:				
Captain..............	Lewis Miller............	Snyder........	Mar. 8, 1865,	....
First Lieutenant....	John H Lewis..........	...Do.........	Mar. 8, 1865,	To Captain Company C......
Do............	Aaron K. Gift..........	...Do.........	June 1, 1865,	....
Second Lieutenant..	Aaron K. Gift..........	...Do.........	Mar. 8, 1865,	To First Lieutenant...........
Do............	Alexander G. Rohbach,	...Do.........	June 1, 1865,	....
Company E:				
Captain..............	William H. Wolfe.......	Northumberland,	Mar. 14, 1865,	....
First Lieutenant....	Henry M. Spayd.......	..........Do	Mar. 14, 1865,	....
Second Lieutenant..	James T. M'Gregor....	..........Do	Mar. 14, 1865,	Discharged May 12, 1865 ......
Company F:				
Captain..............	Garvin A. M'Lain......	Indiana	Mar. 11, 1865,	Discharged May 8, 1865......
Do............	John Kinter.............	...Do...	May 9, 1865,	....
First Lieutenant....	John Kinter.............	...Do...	Mar. 11, 1865,	To Captain.................
Do............	John N. Williams.......	Westmoreland ...	May 9, 1865,	....
Second Lieutenant..	John N. Williams.......	......Do	Mar. 11, 1865,	To First Lieutenant...........
Do............	Matthew Ray...........	Indiana	May 9, 1865,	....
Do............	George Creveling	Philadelphia...	May 9, 1865,	....
Company G:				
Captain..............	William J. Barb........	Adams.........	Mar. 15, 1865,	....
First Lieutenant....	Jacob Lohr.............	...Do..........	Mar. 15, 1865,	....
Second Lieutenant..	Charles Helfrich........	Berks..........	Mar. 15, 1865,	Honorably discharged June 2, 1865 ......
Company H:				
Captain..............	Michael Hellinger.......	Allegheny......	June 1, 1865,	....
Second Lieutenant..	Moritz Strauss.........	......Do	June 1, 1865,	....
Company I:				
Captain..............	Charles Neidhart.......	Allegheny......	June 1, 1865,	....

OFFICERS OF THE 78th REGIMENT, INFANTRY.

RANK.	NAME.	CO. OF RESIDENCE.	DATE OF RANK.	REMARKS.
Lieutenant Colonel..	Charles Knerr............	Luzerne.........	Mar. 9, 1865,	
Major...................	Wm. S. Moorhead......	Philadelphia....	July 4, 1865,	
Adjutant................	Frederick R. Smith....	York..............	Apr. 25, 1865,	
Quartermaster.........	Philemon M. Hicks....	Blair..............	Jan. 15, 1865,	
Company A:				
Captain.................	Aaron C. Mills...........	Lawrence........	Jan. 1, 1865,	Honorably disch'd, to date Mar. 10, 1865.
Do.......................	Jesse R. Sitler...........	Crawford.........	Mar. 11, 1865,	To Captain............
First Lieutenant......	Jesse R. Sitler...........	....Do.............	Jan. 1, 1865,	
Do.......................	Thomas J. Armstrong..	Westmoreland...	Mar. 11, 1865,	
Second Lieutenant..	Robert Biddle............	Centre............	Mar. 11, 1865,	
Company-B:				
Captain.................	William J. Brady.......	Clearfield........	May 6, 1865,	
Second Lieutenant..	Samuel Mohannan......	Mercer............	May 6, 1865,	
Company C:				
Captain.................	John M'Nevin............	Blair..............	Jan. 1, 1865,	
First Lieutenant......	Joseph Harlin............	...Do...............	Jan. 1, 1865,	
Second Lieutenant..	Benjamin White.........	...Do...............	Mar. 10, 1865,	
Company D:				
Captain.................	Luther Y. Diller.........	York..............	July 1, 1865,	To Captain............
First Lieutenant......	Luther Y. Diller.........	...Do...............	Nov. 26, 1864,	
Do.......................	James E Gordon.........	...Do...............	July 1, 1865,	To First Lieutenant...
Second Lieutenant..	James E. Gordon........	...Do...............	Mar. 10, 1865,	
Do.......................	Joseph A. Slagle........	...Do...............	July 1, 1865,	

EXECUTIVE MILITARY DEPARTMENT. 73

....	....	....	...., ...	....
First Lieutenant...	Charles B. Lindsey.....	Venango.	Jan. 1, 1865,	....
Second Lieutenant...	Charles Benseman......	Schuylkill........	Mar. 13, 1865,	....
Company F:				
Captain............	Thomas L. M'Glathery,	Blair	Nov. 26, 1864,	....
Do	James H. M'Divitt.....	Fayette	Jan. 15, 1865,	....
Do	William Blanck, Jr......	Philadelphia.....	June 13, 1865,	To Captain......
First Lieutenant...	James H. M'Divitt.....	Fayette...........	Nov. 26, 1864,	To Captain ......
Do...............	William Blanck, Jr......	Philadelphia.....	Jan. 15, 1865,	....
Do...............	John Hubert............	Blair...............	June 13, 1865,	....
Do...............	James M. Null..........	Allegheny.........	July 1, 1865,	....
Second Lieutenant.	John Shay..............	....Do	July 1, 1865,	....
Do	John Hubert............	Blair...............	Mar. 13, 1865,	....
Company G:				
First Lieutenant...	Isaac Allen	Indiana...........	Jan. 1, 1865,	....
Second Lieutenant.	James S. Harman	Westmoreland...	Mar. 10, 1865,	....
Company H:				
First Lieutenant ...	Peter Houser..........	Dauphin..........	Jan. 1, 1865,	....
Do	David Davis............	Luzerne...........	July 1, 1865,	....
Do...............	David Davis............	....Do............	Mar. 13, 1865,	To First Lieutenant.
Second Lieutenant.	Henry Huffer..........	Dauphin..........	July 1, 1865,	....
Do...............				
Company I:				
Captain............	Harrison Stair.........	York..............	Jan. 1, 1865,	....
First Lieutenant ...	Paris Rudisill..........	Lancaster	Jan. 1, 1865,	....
Second Lieutenant...	Jer. W. Morningstar...	York..............	Mar. 13, 1865,	....
Company K:				
Captain............	Charles Evans.........	Union..............	July 1, 1865,	....
First Lieutenant.....	Henry O. Shelky........	Fayette...........	July 1, 1865,	....

OFFICERS OF THE 77th REGIMENT, INFANTRY.

RANK.	NAME.	CO. OF RESIDENCE.	DATE OF RANK.	REMARKS.
Lieutenant Colonel..	Alexander Phillips......	Luzerne.........	Mar. 25, 1865	Mustered out as Major May 8, 1865 ......
Do............	William A. Robinson...	Allegheny......	May 22, 1865,	
Major...............	William A. Robinson...	......Do.........	Mar. 25, 1865,	To Lieutenant Colonel...........
Do............	Joseph J. Lawson.......	......Do.........	May 27, 1865,	
Quartermaster........	J. Orlando Brookbank.	Cambria.........	Sept. 21, 1865,	
Company A :				
Captain.............	Washington Skinner....	Franklin.........	July 8, 1865,	
First Lieutenant.....	Frederick Sharp	......Do.........	July 8, 1865,	Deceased........
Do............	David F. Daihl........	......Do.........	Aug. 3, 1865,	
Second Lieutenant...	William H. Willet......	......Do.........	April 6, 1865,	
Do............	William Eaker...........	......Do.........	June 19, 1865,	
Company B :				
Captain.............	Frank M. Kreps.........	Westmoreland...	Jan. 24, 1865,	Must'd out as First Lieut. Dec. 31, 1864.
First Lieutenant.....	George S. Drake.........	Allegheny......	Jan. 24, 1865,	
Company C :				
Captain.............	Samuel S. Gillman......	Huntingdon.....	May 22, 1864,	
First Lieutenant.....	Samuel S. Gillman	......Do.........	Dec. 16, 1864,	To Captain...........
Do............	Silas M. Kline...........	Allegheny......	May 22, 1864,	
Second Lieutenant...	Silas M. Kline...........	......Do.........	Dec. 16, 1864,	To First Lieutenant ....
Do............	John T. Baldwin.........	Juniata.........	May 22, 1864,	
Company D :				
Captain.............	Thomas G. Cochrane ...	Franklin	Dec. 16, 1864,	
Do............	James Shaw..............	Allegheny......	Mar. 14, 1864,	

EXECUTIVE MILITARY DEPARTMENT. 75

First Lieutenant......	Arthur Bennett..........	Franklin..........	Dec. 16, 1864,	
Do...................	Edward Noble...........	Allegheny.......	Mar. 14, 1864,	
Second Lieutenant...	John A. Gilliland........	......Do	Mar. 14, 1864,	
Company E :				
Captain................	Sidney J. Branff.........	Allegheny.......	Mar. 13, 1865,	
First Lieutenant.....	John D. Richards........	......Do	Mar. 13, 1865,	
Second Lieutenant...	George M'Knight........	......Do	Mar. 13, 1865,	
Company F :				
Captain................	Daniel Shock.............	Blair.............	Mar. 7, 1865,	
First Lieutenant.....	Miles Zentmyer..........	Huntingdon	Mar. 7, 1865,	
Second Lieutenant...	J. Orlando Brookbank..	Cambria.........	Mar. 7, 1865,	To Quartermaster......
Do...................	George Deihl..............	Blair.............	Sept. 21, 1865,	
Company G :				
Captain................	David Garbet.............	Luzerne..........	May 17, 1864,	
Do...................	Edward Morgan..........	....Do............	June 19, 1865,	
First Lieutenant.....	Edward Morgan..........	......Do	May 17, 1864,	To Captain.............
Do...................	William Watkins.........	......Do	June 19, 1865,	
Second Lieutenant...	William Watkins.........	......Do	May 17, 1864,	To First Lieutenant....
Do...................	John Grieson..............	......Do	June 19, 1865,	
Company H :				
Captain................	Paul F. Rohrbacker.....	Lawrence	Feb. 18, 1865,	
First Lieutenant.....	John C. Mapes	......Do	Feb. 18, 1865,	
Second Lieutenant...	James B. Andrews.......	......Do	Feb. 18, 1865,	
Company I :				
Captain................	John Bell...................	Dauphin..........	Mar. 7, 1865,	
First Lieutenant.....	Henry C. Demming.......	......Do	Mar. 7, 1865,	
Second Lieutenant...	Joseph E. Rhoads........	......Do	Mar. 7, 1865,	

SEVENTY-SEVENTH REGIMENT—Continued.

RANK.	NAME.	CO. OF RESIDENCE.	DATE OF RANK.	REMARKS.
Company K:				
Captain	James A. Haas	Lancaster	Mar. 12, 1865	
First Lieutenant	Jacob Pontz	Do	Mar. 12, 1865	
Second Lieutenant	Jefferson White	Do	Mar. 12, 1865	

OFFICERS OF THE 78th REGIMENT, INFANTRY.

RANK.	NAME.	CO. OF RESIDENCE.	DATE OF RANK.	REMARKS.
Colonel...............	Augustus B. Bonnaffon,	Allegheny.........	Mar. 11, 1865,	....
Lieutenant Colonel,	Henry W. Torbett......	Armstrong........	Mar. 11, 1865,	....
Major.................	Robert M. Smith........	....Do.............	Mar. 11, 1865,	....
Adjutant..............	A. W. Smith.............	......Do............	Mar. 30, 1865,	....
Quartermaster......	William B. M'Cue......	......Do............	Mar. 11, 1865,	....
Company A:				
Captain...............	David A. Rankin......	Indiana............	Mar. 11, 1865,	....
First lieutenant.....	William B. Irvin......	Armstrong........	Mar. 11, 1865,	....
Second Lieutenant..	John M Fleming......	....Do.............	Mar. 11, 1865,	....
Company B:				
Captain................	Andrew Brown.........	Armstrong	Mar. 11, 1865,	....
Do	Bernard Keigan........	Clarion............	July 27, 1865,	To Captain......
First Lieutenant ...	Bernard Keigan........	....Do	Mar. 11, 1865,	....
Do	Wm. H. H. Step........	Armstrong	July 27, 1865,	....
Second Lieutenant.	Wm. H. H. Step........	....Do	Mar. 11, 1865,	To First Lieutenant......
Do	Peter Keck..............	Clarion............	July 27, 1865,	....
Company C:				
Captain..............	Absalom B. Selheimer.	Mifflin	Feb. 18, 1865,	....
First Lieutenant....	John S. M'Kwen......	....Do	Feb. 18, 1865,	....
Second Lieutenant.	Samuel Eisenbise......	....Do	Feb. 18, 1865,	....
Company D:				
Captain................	John A. Swartz.........	Cumberland......	Feb. 18, 1865,	....
First Lieutenant....	Washington L. Stoey...	....Do	Feb. 18, 1865,	....
Second Lieutenant.	Samuel M Mitchell....	Dauphin...........	Feb. 18, 1865,	....

SEVENTY-EIGHTH REGIMENT—Continued.

RANK.	NAME.	CO. OF RESIDENCE.	DATE OF RANK.	REMARKS.
Company E:				
Captain	Robert J. Boggs	Butler	Feb. 26, 1865,	
First Lieutenant	Alexander Gillespie	Do	Feb. 26, 1865,	Resigned June 10, 1865.
Do	Lewis Gantz	Do	June 10, 1865,	
Second Lieutenant	Lewis Gantz	Do	Feb. 26, 1865,	To First Lieutenant.
Do	Charles Hoffman	Do	June 10, 1865,	
Company F:				
Captain	James L. Graham	Allegheny	Feb. 27, 1865,	
First Lieutenant	Thomas Nelson	Do	Feb. 28, 1865,	
Second Lieutenant	Walter Reynolds	Do	Feb. 27, 1865,	
Company G:				
Captain	David S. Cook	Allegheny	Mar. 2, 1865,	
First Lieutenant	Isaac Reno	Mercer	Mar. 2, 1865,	
Do	James R. Cowden	Lawrence	May 25, 1865,	
Second Lieutenant	James R. Cowden	Do	Mar. 2, 1865,	To First Lieutenant.
Do	Benjamin Craven	Do	May 25, 1865,	
Company H:				
Captain	Paul Crawford	Allegheny	Mar. 4, 1865,	
First Lieutenant	Joseph B. Bown	Do	Mar. 4, 1865,	
Second Lieutenant	Joseph H. Rubincam	Do	Mar. 4, 1865,	
Company I:				
Captain	Charles D. Wiley	Allegheny	Mar. 2, 1865,	
First Lieutenant	John M'Roberts	Do	Mar. 2, 1865,	

Second Lieutenant..	George B. M'Nulty.....	Allegheny.........	April 26, 1865,
Company K :			
Captain...............	John Brewster,........		Mar. 2, 1865,
First Lieutenant.....	David G. Enyeart.......		Mar. 2, 1865,
Second Lieutenant..	Milton H. Sangree......		Mar. 2, 1865,

OFFICERS OF THE 79th REGIMENT, INFANTRY.

RANK.	NAME.	CO. OF RESIDENCE	DATE OF RANK	REMARKS.
Major	John S. McBride	Lancaster	Dec. 20, 1864,	
Company A:				
Captain	Edward McCaffery	Lancaster	Dec. 20, 1864,	Honorably discharged, to take effect May [15, 1865.]
First Lieutenant	George Huffnagle	Do	Jan. 6, 1865,	
Second Lieutenant	Christian M. Greaff	Do	Mar. 29, 1865,	
Company C:				
Captain	Cyrus L. Eckert	Lancaster	Dec. 20, 1864,	
Second Lieutenant	Jacob K. Snyder	Do	April 1, 1865,	
Company D:				
Second Lieutenant	Luke P. Beazell	Lancaster	April 1, 1865,	
Company E:				
Second Lieutenant	Stephen S. Clair	Lancaster	Mar. 29, 1865,	
Company F:				
Second Lieutenant	John Myers	Lancaster	Mar. 29, 1865,	
Company G:				
First Lieutenant	James H. Marshall	Lancaster	Dec. 18, 1864,	
Second Lieutenant	Henry Ransing	Do	Mar. 29, 1865,	
Company H:				
Second Lieutenant	Frederic Rice	Lancaster	Mar. 29, 1865,	

Company I:			
First Lieutenant....	George Greiner.........	Lancaster.........	Dec. 18, 1864,
Second Lieutenant.	Daniel A. Zook.......	......Do........	Mar. 29, 1865,
Company K:			
First Lieutenant....	William H. Pool.........	Lancaster.........	April 1, 1865,
Second Lieutenant.	Philip Metzgar.........	......Do........	April 1, 1865,

OFFICERS OF THE 80th REGIMENT, SEVENTH CAVALRY.

RANK.	NAME.	CO. OF RESIDENCE.	DATE OF RANK.	REMARKS.
Colonel	Charles C. M'Cormick	Northumberland	Dec. 1, 1864	
Lieutenant Colonel	James F. Andress	Chester	Dec. 22, 1864	
Major	Cyrus Newlin	Philadelphia	Oct. 15, 1864	
Do	Benjamin S. Dart	Bradford	Dec. 6, 1864	
Do	Charles L. Greno	Do	Dec. 22, 1864	
Do	Uriah C. Hartranft	Northumberland	July 24, 1865	
Adjutant	William M. Watts	Cumberland	Mar. 2, 1865	
Quartermaster	George B. F. Kitchen	Schuylkill	Nov. 29, 1864	To Captain Company A
Do	Charles Trego	Northumberland	July 24, 1865	
Commissary	George T. Frazier	Butler	Dec. 20, 1864	
Do	Michael Breckbill	Montour	July 24, 1865	
Company A:				
Captain	George B. F. Kitchen	Schuylkill	July 24, 1865	
First Lieutenant	Edward L. Shutt		Dec. 1, 1864	
Second Lieutenant	Peter F. Kelly	Schuylkill	Dec. 20, 1864	
Company B:				
Captain	Jonas F. Long	Berks	Dec. 15, 1864	
First Lieutenant	John F. Somers	Chester	Dec. 15, 1864	
Second Lieutenant	Edward P. Imhoff	Cumberland	Dec. 15, 1864	To Captain Company E
Do	John Rich	Schuylkill	Dec. 20, 1864	
Company C:				
Captain	Samuel C. Dixon	Chester	Dec. 6, 1864	
First Lieutenant	A. J. B. Dart		Oct. 1, 1864	
Second Lieutenant	William Sims		Dec. 1, 1864	

EXECUTIVE MILITARY DEPARTMENT.

Company D:				
Captain	John Schuyler	Northumberland	Dec. 1, 1864	
Do	Uriah C. Hartranft	Do	Dec. 20, 1864	To Major
Do	Samuel C. Bryson	Do	July 24, 1865	
First Lieutenant	Jesse B. Rank	Do	Dec. 1, 1864	
Do	Samuel C. Bryson	Do	Dec. 20, 1864	To Captain
Do	Wm. A. Hartranft	Do	July 24, 1865	
Second Lieutenant	Samuel C. Bryson	Do	Dec. 1, 1864	To First Lieutenant
Do	Michael Breckbill	Do	Dec. 20, 1864	To Commissary
Do	Samuel M Blain	Do	July 24, 1865	
Company E:				
Captain	George F. Steahlen	Schuylkill	Nov 1, 1864	
Do	Edward P. Imhoff	Cumberland	Dec. 20, 1864	
First Lieutenant	William E. Hayes	Clinton	July 24, 1865	
Second Lieutenant	William E. Hayes	Do	Dec. 20, 1864	To First Lieutenant
Do	Henry L. Bricker	Do	July 24, 1865	
Company F:				
Captain	Richard H. Fisk	Schuylkill	Oct. 15, 1864	
Do	William Jenkins	Do	July 24, 1865	
First Lieutenant	Valentine K. Boyer	Do	Dec. 1, 1864	
Do	George Nutz	Do	July 24, 1865	Resigned March 29, 1865
Second Lieutenant	William Jenkins	Do	Dec. 1, 1864	
Do	Daniel Seigfried	Do	July 24, 1865	
Company G:				
Captain	Wash. M. Hinkson	Chester	Feb. 8, 1865	Honorably discharged for disability, May [14, 1865.
Do	Wash. M. Hinkson	Do	May 15, 1865	
First Lieutenant	William N. Grier	Do	Oct. 15, 1864	
Company H:				
Captain	Clinton W. Boone	Northumberland	Dec. 22, 1864	Hon. disch., to take effect May 15, 1865.

EIGHTIETH REGIMENT—Continued.

RANK.	NAME.	CO. OF RESIDENCE.	DATE OF RANK.	REMARKS.
Captain	Clinton W. Boone	Northumberland,	May 15, 1865,	
First Lieutenant	John Getchy		Dec. 22, 1864,	Resignation accepted March 6, 1865
Do	Albert S. Watson	Northumberland,	Mar. 7, 1865,	
Second Lieutenant.	John Getchy		Nov. 1, 1864,	To First Lieutenant
Do	Albert S. Watson	Northumberland,	Dec. 22, 1864,	To First Lieutenant
Do	Thomas M'Gowen	Allegheny	Mar. 7, 1865,	
Company I:				
Captain	Cyrus L. Conner	Fayette	Mar. 1, 1865,	
First Lieutenant	George W. Starry	Dauphin	Dec. 1, 1864,	Resignation accepted Feb. 28, 1865
Do	Isaac S. Keith	Cumberland	Mar. 1, 1865,	
Second Lieutenant.	Cyrus L. Conner	Fayette	Dec. 1, 1864,	To Captain
Do	James T. Mitchell	Dauphin	Mar. 1, 1865,	
Company K:				
Captain	Frederick H. Geety	Dauphin	Nov. 5, 1864,	
Do	William H. Collins	Fayette	July 24, 1865,	
First Lieutenant	William H. Collins	Do	Dec. 1, 1864,	To Captain
Do	Wm. O. Bateman	Philadelphia	July 24, 1865,	
Second Lieutenant.	Wm. O. Bateman	Do	Dec. 1, 1864,	To First Lieutenant
Do	George M. Herr	Dauphin	July 24, 1865,	
Company L:				
Captain	William Wren	Schuylkill	Dec. 1, 1864,	
First Lieutenant	Otis Jerould	Tioga	Dec. 1, 1864,	
Second Lieutenant.	Henry H. Snyder	Schuylkill	Dec. 1, 1864,	

Company M:

Captain............	Charles Brandt............	Allegheny.........	Dec. 1, 1864,
First Lieutenant.....	Alexander M. Parker....	Cumberland	Dec. 1, 1864,
Second Lieutenant..	Charles Waltz............	....	Dec. 1, 1864,

OFFICERS OF THE 81st REGIMENT, INFANTRY.

RANK.	NAME.	CO. OF RESIDENCE.	DATE OF RANK.	REMARKS.
Adjutant...........	Robert J. Ross.........	Philadelphia.....	June 29, 1865,	....
Quartermaster......	Jacob A. Hollinger.....	Lancaster	June 29, 1865,	....
Chaplain...........	Walter R. Whitney....	Bedford	Mar. 3, 1865,	....
Company A:				
Captain............	Joseph S. Webb.........	Carbon...........	April 8, 1865,	....
First Lieutenant ...	Joseph S. Webb.........	...Do............	Mar. 5, 1865,	To Captain........
Do	John Ward.............	Philadelphia.....	April 8, 1865,	....
Second Lieutenant..	John Ward	......Do..........	Mar 28, 1865,	To First Lieutenant....
Do	Isaac N. Wilson........	......Do..........	April 8, 1865,	....
Do	Lawrence Davenport....	......Do..........	June 29, 1865,	....
Company B:				
Captain............	John Bond.............	Carbon...........	Jan. 7, 1865,	....
Do	William Hanna.........	Philadelphia.....	April 8, 1865,	....
First Lieutenant ...	William Hanna.........	......Do..........	Jan. 7, 1865,	To Captain........
Do	John Graham..........	......Do..........	April 8, 1865,	....
Second Lieutenant,.	William Hanna.........	......Do..........	Dec. 7, 1864,	To First Lieutenant....
Do	John Graham..........	......Do..........	Mar. 28, 1865,	To First Lieutenant....
Do	George Williams........	......Do..........	June 29, 1865,	....
Company C:				
Captain............	Horatio B. Hackett.....	Philadelphia.....	April 19, 1865,	....
First Lieutenant ...	John Hughes	......Do..........	Nov. 25, 1864,	....
Do	Horatio B. Hackett.....	......Do..........	April 17, 1865,	To Captain........
Do	Thomas Gallagher......	Carbon...........	June 29, 1865,	....
Second Lieutenant..	Horatio B. Hackett.....	Philadelphia.....	Nov. 25, 1864,	To First Lieutenant....

EXECUTIVE MILITARY DEPARTMENT.

Second Lieutenant..	Thomas Gallagher.......	Carbon........	April 17, 1865,	To First Lieutenant...............
Do........	William M'Kensie.......	Philadelphia......	June 29, 1865,	
Company D:				
Captain........	Robert Thompson.......	Philadelphia.....	June 29, 1865,	
First Lieutenant...	Charles M'Bride........	Do.......	Dec. 22, 1864,	Discharged, to date May 8, 1865...
Do........	Thomas Nugent.........	Do.......	June 29, 1865,	
Second Lieutenant..	Robert Thompson.......	Do.......	Jan. 7, 1865,	To Captain...........
Do........	William Francis........	Do.......	June 29, 1865,	
Company E:				
First Lieutenant...	John France............	Philadelphia.....	Dec. 22, 1864,	
Do........	John M'Fadden.........	Do.......	June 29, 1865,	
Second Lieutenant..	John Adams...........	Do.......	Jan. 7, 1865,	
Do........	James Flemming........	Do.......	June 29, 1865,	
Company F:				
Captain........	Henry Wilson..........	Philadelphia.....	April 6, 1865,	
First Lieutenant...	Daniel Deno...........	Do.......	Nov. 25, 1864,	Discharged, to date March 14, 1865...
Do........	John Armstrong........	Do.......	June 29, 1865,	
Second Lieutenant..	Henry Wilson..........	Do.......	Nov. 25, 1864,	To Captain...........
Do........	John Johnson..........	Do.......	June 29, 1865,	
Company I:				
Captain........	Nathan F. Marsh.......	Philadelphia.....	Jan. 7, 1865,	
First Lieutenant...	Henry Paltzgrove.......	Carbon........	Jan. 7, 1865,	
Second Lieutenant..	Henry Paltzgrove.......	Do.......	May 13, 1864,	To First Lieutenant...............
Do........	Stewart M'Intosh.......	Do.......	Jan. 7, 1865,	
Company K:				
Second Lieutenant..	Washington Setzer.....	Luzerne........	Jan. 7, 1865,	

OFFICERS OF THE 82d REGIMENT, INFANTRY.

RANK.	NAME.	CO. OF RESIDENCE.	DATE OF RANK.	REMARKS.
Lieutenant Colonel.	James R. Neiler	Philadelphia	Nov. 26, 1864,	
Major	William Clark	Do	Jan. 22, 1865,	Honorably discharged, to take effect May 15, 1865.
Company A:				
Captain	Thomas H. Marston	Philadelphia	Nov. 26, 1864,	
First Lieutenant	John C. A. Stackhouse	Do	Dec. 1, 1864,	
Second Lieutenant	James Stapleton	Schuylkill	Dec. 18, 1864,	
Company C:				
Second Lieutenant	Charles Williamson	Philadelphia	Dec. 14, 1864,	
Company D:				
Captain	George W. Waterhouse	Philadelphia	Nov. 26, 1864,	
First Lieutenant	Henry C. Norma	Do	Nov. 26, 1864,	
Second Lieutenant	William H. Dilks	Do	Nov. 26, 1864,	[1865.
Do	Francis Hermana	Do	Jan. 12, 1865,	Honorably discharged, to date May 15,
Company E:				
First Lieutenant	Casper Miller	Philadelphia	Jan. 12, 1865,	
Second Lieutenant	John Gallagher	Do	Jan. 12, 1865,	
Company F:				
Second Lieutenant	John F. M'Kernan	Philadelphia	Jan. 12, 1865,	
Company I:				
Captain	Stephen Palmore	Philadelphia	Jan. 12, 1865,	
Second Lieutenant	Charles G. Fell	Do	Jan. 12, 1865,	

EXECUTIVE MILITARY DEPARTMENT. 89

Company A.			
Captain	John F. Reen	Philadelphia	Jan. 12, 1865,
First Lieutenant	William H. Myers	York	Jan. 12, 1865,
Second Lieutenant	Russell P. Howard	Philadelphia	Jan. 12, 1865,

ANNUAL REPORT OF THE

OFFICERS OF THE 83d REGIMENT, INFANTRY.

RANK.	NAME.	CO. OF RESIDENCE.	DATE OF RANK.	REMARKS.
Colonel	Chauncey P. Rogers	Erie	Mar. 6, 1865,	
Lieutenant Colonel	William O. Colt	Do	Mar. 6, 1865,	
Major	William O. Colt	Do	Dec 26, 1864,	To Lieutenant Colonel
Do	W. H. Dunbar	Philadelphia	Mar. 6, 1865,	
Adjutant	B. M. Frank	Dauphin	May 5, 1865,	
Quartermaster	George M. Boal	Centre	Mar. 10, 1865,	
Company A:				
Captain	Edward L. Whittlesey	Erie	Feb. 17, 1865,	
First Lieutenant	Wilkes S. Colt	Do	Feb. 17, 1865,	
Second Lieutenant	James A. Moore	Erie	Dec. 17, 1864,	
Do	Wilkes S. Colt	Erie	Feb. 17, 1865,	To First Lieutenant
Do	David C. Gray	Do	June 23, 1865,	
Company B:				
Captain	A. J. M'Kee	Erie	Feb. 17, 1865,	
First Lieutenant	Harrison Raymond	Do	Feb. 17, 1865,	
Second Lieutenant	Harrison Raymond	Do	Feb. 17, 1865,	To First Lieutenant
Do	Joseph H. Bowman	Crawford	June 23, 1865,	
Company C:				
First Lieutenant	Charles H. Hubbell	Erie	June 10, 1865,	
Second Lieutenant	Samuel L. Fluke	Erie	Dec. 17, 1864,	Resigned February 4, 1865
Do	Charles H. Hubbell	Erie	Feb. 17, 1865,	To First Lieutenant
Do	Daniel B. Foote	Do	June 10, 1865,	

EXECUTIVE MILITARY DEPARTMENT. 91

Company D:				
First Lieutenant....	Isaac Keck.............		Dec. 17, 1864,	
Second Lieutenant..	Abijah H. Burnett.....		Dec. 17, 1864,	
Company E:				
Captain................	Peter Grace............	Mercer.......	Feb. 17, 1865,	
First Lieutenant....	Peter Grace............	Do...........	Dec. 17, 1864,	To Captain.
Do................	Wm. H. M'Gill.........	Venango......	Feb. 17, 1865,	
Second Lieutenant..	Wm. H. M'Gill.........	Do...........	Dec. 17, 1864,	To First Lieutenant.
Do................	James C. Percival.....	Do...........	Feb. 17, 1865,	
Company F:				
Second Lieutenant..	William L. Bennett....	Erie..........	Feb. 17, 1865,	
Company G:				
Captain................	Casper Gang...........	Allegheny....	Mar. 2, 1865,	
First Lieutenant....	Lewis Broerman.......	Do...........	Mar. 2, 1865,	
Do................	Charles G. Sautter.....	Do...........	June 23, 1865,	
Second Lieutenant..	Charles G. Sautter.....	Do...........	Mar. 2, 1865,	To First Lieutenant.
Do................	William Gust...........	Do...........	June 23, 1865,	
Company H:				
Captain................	Henry W. Horback.....	Allegheny....	Mar. 1, 1865,	
Do................	Franklin Sweet.........	Clarion.......	June 23, 1865,	To Captain.
First Lieutenant....	Franklin Sweet.........	Do...........	Mar. 1, 1865,	
Do................	John Little, Jr..........	Allegheny....	June 23, 1865,	To First Lieutenant.
Second Lieutenant..	John Little, Jr..........	Do...........	Mar. 1, 1865,	
Do................	Joseph C. Beck.........	Do...........	June 23, 1865,	
Company I:				
Captain................	Robert W. M'Cartney..	Dauphin......	Mar. 1, 1865,	
First Lieutenant....	Louis F. Mason........	Centre........	Mar. 1, 1865,	
Second Lieutenant..	Abraham Frauenthal...	Dauphin......	Mar. 1, 1865,	

EIGHTY-THIRD REGIMENT—Continued.

RANK.	NAME.	CO. OF RESIDENCE.	DATE OF RANK.	REMARKS.
Company K:				
Captain............	George W. Huff............	Dauphin............	Mar. 11, 1865,	....
First Lieutenant.....	John Deetrick............	....Do............	Mar. 11, 1865,	....
Second Lieutenant..	Benjamin M. Frank.....	Blair............	Mar. 11, 1865,	....
Do	David O. Ritter............	Dauphin............	June 23, 1865,	....

OFFICERS OF THE 87th REGIMENT, INFANTRY.

RANK.	NAME.	CO. OF RESIDENCE.	DATE OF RANK.	REMARKS.
Colonel	Walter S. Franklin	York	Jan. 31, 1865,	Declined to be mustered
Do	James Tearney	Lancaster	May 10, 1865,	
Lieutenant Colonel	Noah G. Ruhl	York	Mar. 17, 1865,	Declined to be mustered
Do	Samuel S. Bulford	Washington	June 15, 1865,	
Major	Findlay J. Thomas	Adams	June 15, 1865,	
Adjutant	William K. Parker	Dauphin	June 15, 1865,	
Company A :				
Captain	George J. Chalfant	York	May 10, 1865,	
First Lieutenant	Lewis Rasch	Do	May 10, 1865,	
Company B :				
Captain	Zepheniah Hersh		Jan. 3, 1865,	Not mustered
First Lieutenant	Henry Epley	York	May 10, 1865,	
Do	John M. Yeager	Adams	June 15, 1865,	
Second Lieutenant	David N. Thomas	Do	June 15, 1865,	
Company C :				
Captain	Findlay J. Thomas	Adams	Jan. 3, 1865,	To Major
Do	Jonathan J. Keasey	York	June 15, 1865,	
First Lieutenant	Jonathan J. Keasey	Do	May 10, 1865,	To Captain
Second Lieutenant	Andrew J. Wetzel	Perry	June 18, 1865,	
Company D :				
Captain	Andrew G. Shull	York	May 10, 1865,	Discharged as First Lieut. June 1, 1865.
Do	Jacob R. Nonemaker	Do	June 6, 1865,	

EIGHTY-SEVENTH REGIMENT—Continued.

RANK.	NAME.	CO. OF RESIDENCE.	DATE OF RANK.	REMARKS.
First Lieutenant....	Jacob R. Nonemaker....	York............	May 10, 1865,	To Captain............
Do..................	Joseph F. Welsh........	..Do............	June 6, 1865,	....
Second Lieutenant..	Henry Stine............	....Do..........	June 6, 1865,	....
Company E:				
Captain.............	Charles J. Fox.........	York............	May 10, 1865,	....
First Lieutenant....	Issac J. Simmons.......	..Do............	June 15, 1865,	....
Second Lieutenant..	Henry A. Zercher.......	Lancaster......	June 15, 1865,	....
Company F:				
Captain.............	James R. M'Cormac.....	Allegheny......	Mar. 6, 1865,	....
First Lieutenant....	Robert Brown	......Do.........	Mar. 6, 1865,	....
Do..................	James S. Brocker	Cambria.........	June 15, 1865,	....
Second Lieutenant..	Nicholas Kelly.........	Allegheny......	Mar. 6, 1865,	....
Do..................	Henry H. Colbaugh.....	......Do.........	June 15, 1865,	....
Company G:				
Captain.............	William H. Trovillo....	Allegheny......	Mar. 7, 1865,	....
First Lieutenant....	Charles Bryson.........	..Do............	Mar. 7, 1865,	....
Second Lieutenant..	Nathan G. Barnhart....	..Do............	Mar. 7, 1865,	....
Company H:				
Captain.............	Samuel S. Bulford......	Washington.....	Mar. 15, 1865,	....
First Lieutenant....	David Cartright........	Lawrence.......	Mar. 15, 1865,	....
Second Lieutenant..	David G. W. Andrews,..	....Do..........	Mar. 15, 1865,	....

EXECUTIVE MILITARY DEPARTMENT. 95

Company I:				
Captain............	Solomon Cover.........	Dauphin.........	Mar. 15, 1865,	....
First Lieutenant....	Caleb Roe.............	Do............	Mar 15, 1865,	....
Do..............	Henry Crist...........	Lebanon........	June 15, 1865,	To First Lieutenant.
Second Lieutenant..	Henry Crist...........	...Do..........	Mar. 15, 1865,	....
Do..............	Joseph A. Cunkle.......	Dauphin.........	June 15, 1865,	....
Company K:				
Captain............	David B. Greenawalt...	Franklin.........	Mar. 17, 1865,	....
First Lieutenant....	Simon H. Foreman.....	...Do..........	Mar 17, 1865,	....
Second Lieutenant..	John C. Brown.........	...Do..........	Mar. 17, 1865,	....

OFFICERS OF THE 88th REGIMENT, INFANTRY.

RANK.	NAME.	CO. OF RESIDENCE.	DATE OF RANK.	REMARKS.
Colonel	Louis Wagner	Philadelphia	Mar. 3, 1863,	
Lieutenant Colonel	Edmund A. Mass	Berks	Mar. 3, 1863,	
Major	Aaron Bright, Jr	Do	Jan. 1, 1865,	
Adjutant	Isaiah M'Intire	Philadelphia	June 14, 1865,	
Company A:				
Captain	Thomas J. Kock		Dec. 4, 1864,	
Do	Daniel W. Ney	Chester	June 14, 1865,	
First Lieutenant	Thomas J. Kock	Chester	Nov. 24, 1864,	To Captain
Do	Daniel W. Ney	Berks	Feb. 20, 1865,	To Captain
Do	George H. Reiff		June 14, 1865,	
Second Lieutenant	Joseph H. Kline	Do	June 14, 1865,	
Company B:				
Captain	Albert Nagle	Berks	Mar. 3, 1865,	
First Lieutenant	Albert Nagle	Do	June 9, 1865,	To Captain
Do	Aaron Myer	Do	Mar. 3, 1865,	
Second Lieutenant	Aaron Myer	Do	June 9, 1865,	To First Lieutenant
Do	Lafayette K. Mohn	Do	Mar. 3, 1865,	
Company C:				
Captain	Robert Thwaits	Philadelphia	Dec. 5, 1864,	
First Lieutenant	Robert Herron	Do	Dec. 5, 1864,	
Second Lieutenant	Nathan L. Jones	Do	June 9, 1865,	
Do	Jonathan E. Rogers	Montgomery	June 14, 1865,	

EXECUTIVE MILITARY DEPARTMENT.

Captain............	James P. Meade......	Philadelphia.....	Dec. 2, 1864,	
First Lieutenant....	Charles Hunter........	....Do......	Aug. 13, 1864,	
Do	John Ewing........	....Do......	June 14, 1865,	To First Lieutenant.....
Second Lieutenant..	John Ewing........	....Do......	June 9, 1865,	
Do	Mortimer Wisham......	....Do......	June 14, 1865,	
Company E:				
Captain............	Edward L. Gilligan.....	Philadelphia.....	Dec. 5, 1864,	
First Lieutenant....	Daniel G. Lehman......	....Do......	Dec. 5, 1864,	
Do	John F. Campbell......	....Do......	June 14, 1865,	To First Lieutenant.....
Second Lieutenant..	John F. Campbell......	....Do......	June 9, 1865,	
Do	Joseph Burris........	....Do......	June 14, 1865,	
Company F:				
Captain............	Richard B. Clevenger.	Philadelphia.....	Dec. 19, 1864,	
First Lieutenant....	Matthew Myers........	....Do......	Mar. 2, 1865,	
Second Lieutenant..	Henry S. Waide	....Do......	Mar. 2, 1865,	
Company G:				
Captain............	Aaron Bright, Jr........	Berks.........	Dec. 4, 1864,	To Major.....
Do	William Huber........	Lehigh........	June 14, 1865,	
First Lieutenant....	William Huber........	....Do.........	Dec. 4, 1864,	To Captain.
Do	Cyrus Soder.........	Berks.........	June 14, 1865,	
Second Lieutenant..	William Truett........	Philadelphia.....	June 14, 1865,	
Company H:				
First Lieutenant....	Jefferson Good........	Berks.........	May 16, 1865,	
Second Lieutenant..	Jefferson Good........	....Do........	May 20, 1865,	To First Lieutenant.....
Do	John Whitmoyer.......	....Do........	May 16, 1865,	
Company I:				
Captain............	Henry J. Copestick....	Philadelphia.....	June 13, 1865,	

7 MILITARY DEPART.

EIGHTY-EIGHTH REGIMENT—Continued.

RANK.	NAME.	CO. OF RESIDENCE.	DATE OF RANK.	REMARKS.
First Lieutenant....	Henry B. O'Neill.........	....	Oct. 19, 1864,	....
Do	Henry D. Evans	Philadelphia......	June 13, 1865,	....
Second Lieutenant..	James K. Shelcup.......	......Do	June 13, 1865,	....
Company K:				
Captain...............	Sylvester H. Martin.....	Philadelphia......	Jan. 30, 1865,	....
Do...	Charles M'Knight........	......Do	June 14, 1865,	....
First Lieutenant	Charles M'Knight........	......Do	Jan. 30, 1865,	To Captain.........
Do...............	Daniel Linsanbigler.....	Montgomery......	June 14, 1865,	....
Second Lieutenant..	Charles C Lambert.....	Philadelphia......	June 14, 1865,	....

OFFICERS OF THE 89th REGIMENT, EIGHTH CAVALRY.

RANK.	NAME.	CO. OF RESIDENCE.	DATE OF RANK.	REMARKS.
Colonel............	William A. Corrie......	Philadelphia.....	July 1, 1865,	....
Lieutenant Colonel.	William A. Corrie......	......Do........	Dec. 20, 1864,	To Colonel..........
Do...............	Robert Oldham..........	......Do........	July 1, 1865,	....
Major..............	Robert Oldham..........	......Do........	Dec. 20, 1864,	To Lieutenant Colonel.......
Do...............	Robert M'Cool..........	......Do........	Dec. 20, 1864,	....
Do...............	Benjamin A. Phifer.....	......Do........	July 1, 1865,	....
Quartermaster.......	Charles M. Clemens.....	....	Dec. 20, 1864,	....
Commissary.........	B. Frank Inman.........	....	Dec. 20, 1864,	Honorably disch'd, to date May 15, 1865.
Do...............	John Galloway..........	Philadelphia.....	July 1, 1865,	....
Company B :				
Captain............	Daniel B. Dykens.......	Lycoming.........	Dec. 20, 1864,	....
Second Lieutenant..	H. S. Graham...........	Union............	Mar. 18, 1865,	....
Company C :				
Captain............	Benjamin A. Phifer.....	Philadelphia.....	Dec. 20, 1864,	To Major........
First Lieutenant...	D. W. Davis............	......Do........	Dec. 20, 1864,	....
Second Lieutenant..	Florrent W. Gigon......	Philadelphia.....	Mar. 10, 1865,	....
Do...............	Isaac Drake............	......Do........	July 1, 1865,	....
Company D :				
Captain............	Charles O. Fitch.......	Philadelphia.....	Jan. 24, 1865,	....
First Lieutenant..	Charles O. Fitch.......	......Do........	Dec. 20, 1864,	To Captain.......
Second Lieutenant..	Andrew Lee.............	......Do........	Dec. 20, 1864,	....
Company F :				
Captain............	Robert M'Cool..........	Philadelphia.....	Oct. 1, 1864,	To Major........

EIGHTY-NINTH REGIMENT—Continued.

RANK.	NAME.	CO. OF RESIDENCE.	DATE OF RANK.	REMARKS.
Captain............	Frank A. Baker.........	Philadelphia......	Dec. 20, 1864,	
First Lieutenant...	Alfred Maxey...........	......Do	June 1, 1865,	
Second Lieutenant.	Wm. E. Bragg..........	......Do	Dec. 20, 1864,	
Company G:				
Captain............	John S. Howard.........	Lycoming.........	Oct. 1, 1864,	
Do	Thomas J. Gregg........	Huntingdon.......	June 5, 1865,	
First Lieutenant...	Robert C. Payne........	Lycoming.........	Dec. 20, 1864,	
Do................	John Snyder............	......Do	June 1, 1865,	Hon. discharged, to date May 15, 1865...
Second Lieutenant.	Frank Craft............	......Do	Dec. 20, 1864,	
Company H:				
Captain............	Thomas A. Davis........	Lycoming.........	Jan. 15, 1865,	
First Lieutenant...	Thomas A. Davis........	......Do	Oct. 1, 1864,	To Captain........
Do	James M'Nichol.........	Philadelphia......	Dec. 20, 1864,	
Second Lieutenant.	George K. Stevens.......	......Do	Dec. 20, 1864,	
Company I:				
Captain............	E. H. Moore............	Philadelphia......	Dec. 20, 1864,	
First Lieutenant...	Samuel Conklin.........	......Do	Dec. 20, 1864,	
Company K:				
Captain............	Clem A. White..........	Philadelphia......	Dec. 20, 1864,	
Do	Lester D. Phelps........	......Do	Mar. 18, 1865,	
First Lieutenant...	Wm. H. Bentz...........	......Do	Mar. 18, 1865,	
Second Lieutenant.	Edward G. Wright.......	......Do	Mar. 18, 1865,	

EXECUTIVE MILITARY DEPARTMENT. 101

OFFICERS OF THE 91st REGIMENT, INFANTRY.

RANK.	NAME.	CO. OF RESIDENCE.	DATE OF RANK.	REMARKS.
Adjutant............	John R. Allen...........	Philadelphia......	April 28, 1865,	
Quartermaster........	Archibald Nimme.......	....	Mar. 11, 1865,	
Company A:				
First Lieutenant.....	William Beaver.........	Philadelphia......	April 28, 1865,	
Company B:				
Captain.............	John C. Partenheimer..	Philadelphia......	Dec. 1, 1864,	
First Lieutenant.....	William Knapp.........	......Do	Dec. 1, 1864,	
Company C:				
Second Lieutenant...	John Maginnis..........	Philadelphia......	April 28, 1865,	
Company D:				
First Lieutenant.....	George McMullen.......	Philadelphia......	Feb. 17, 1865,	
Second Lieutenant...	William H. Chandler...	......Do	April 28, 1865,	
Company E:				
Second Lieutenant...	John J. Griffith........	Philadelphia......	April 28, 1865,	
Company F:				
First Lieutenant.....	Edward Hause..........	Philadelphia......	April 28, 1865,	
Company G:				
Captain.............	William Spangler.......	Philadelphia......	Feb. 17, 1865,	
First Lieutenant.....	Wm. Letourneau.......	......Do	Feb. 17, 1865,	

NINETY-FIRST REGIMENT—Continued.

RANK.	NAME.	CO. OF RESIDENCE.	DATE OF RANK.	REMARKS.
Company H:				
Captain............	George P. Finney......	Philadelphia.....	Dec. 1, 1864,	....
First Lieutenant....	Wm. H. Fraley........	Do	Dec. 1, 1864,	Hon. discharged April 4, 1865....
Do................	Franklin Wolfinger.....	Do	April 28, 1865,	....
Company I:				
First Lieutenant....	Henry W. Erdman.....	Philadelphia.....	Mar. 27, 1865,	....
Second Lieutenant..	George A. Souders.....	Do	April 28, 1865,	....
Company K:				
Captain............	George G. Coster......	Philadelphia.....	April 28, 1865,	....
First Lieutenant....	George G. Coster......	Do	Dec. 1, 1864,	To Captain......................
Do................	John F. Casner........	Do	April 28, 1865,	....

OFFICERS OF THE 92d REGIMENT, NINTH CAVALRY.

RANK.	NAME.	CO. OF RESIDENCE.	DATE OF RANK.	REMARKS.
Major	John F. Miller	Dauphin	May 11, 1865,	
Adjutant	Isaac D. Landis	Cumberland	June 4, 1865,	
Company A:				
Captain	William M. Potter	Perry	Mar. 16, 1865,	
First Lieutenant	Eleazer Michener	Do	Mar. 16, 1865,	
Second Lieutenant	Eleazer Michener	Do	Mar. 16, 1865,	To First Lieutenant.
Do	James B. Hamersly	Lehigh	Mar. 16, 1865,	
Company C:				
Captain	Nathan W. Horton	Luzerne	Sept. 26, 1864,	
First Lieutenant	Lawrence A. Crihuian	Butler	Sept. 26, 1864,	
Second Lieutenant	George Sipe	Cumberland	Sept. 26, 1864,	
Company D:				
Second Lieutenant	Frederick Smith	Luzerne	June 27, 1865,	
Company E:				
Captain	Louis A. Hoke	Lancaster	Apr. 8, 1865,	
First Lieutenant	Jacob Coller	Perry	Apr. 8, 1865,	
Second Lieutenant	John H. Shammo	Dauphin	Apr. 8, 1865,	
Company F:				
First Lieutenant	Theodore Oliver	Northampton	Apr. 8, 1865,	
Do	Samuel W. Schauers	Lancaster	June 16, 1865,	
Second Lieutenant	Samuel W. Schauers	Do	Apr. 8, 1865,	To First Lieutenant.
Do	Elias Brua	Do	June 16, 1865,	

NINETY-SECOND REGIMENT—Continued.

RANK.	NAME.	CO. OF RESIDENCE.	DATE OF RANK.	REMARKS.
Company G:				
Captain............	Thomas U. Culbertson,	Cumberland......	June 16, 1865,	
First Lieutenant....	William Keiser..........	Dauphin..........	June 16, 1865,	
Second Lieutenant..	Joseph Dunlap...........	Lancaster........	June 16, 1865,	
Company H:				
Second Lieutenant..	Urias Shaffer............	Cumberland......	June 4, 1865,	
Company K:				
Captain............	William Guyer..........	Cumberland......	June 16, 1865,	
First Lieutenant....	William Wheeler........	Luzerne...........	June 16, 1865,	
Second Lieutenant..	John F. Burke...........	....Do	June 16, 1865,	
Company M:				
Captain............	Doctor A. Shelp........	Luzerne...........	Aug. 1, 1864,	
First Lieutenant....	Andrew M. Clarke......	....Do	Aug. 1, 1864,	
Do	William Irvin............	Blair.............	June 16, 1865,	
Second Lieutenant..	William Irvin............	....Do	Aug 1, 1864,	To First Lieutenant......
Do	George W. Kuhn........	Huntingdon	June 16, 1865,	

OFFICERS OF THE 93d REGIMENT, INFANTRY.

RANK.	NAME.	CO. OF RESIDENCE.	DATE OF RANK.	REMARKS.
Colonel	Charles W. Eckman	Montour	Aug. 26, 1863,	
Lieutenant Colonel	Daniel C Keller	Berks	Dec. 18, 1864,	
Major	John Fritz	Lebanon	Dec. 18, 1864,	
Adjutant	John B. Dewees	Berks	Mar. 4, 1865,	
Company A:				
Captain	Washington Horn	Lebanon	Mar. 26, 1865,	
First Lieutenant	David R. P. M'Caully	Do	Mar. 26, 1865,	
Second Lieutenant	David R. P. M'Caully	Do	Oct. 2, 1864,	To First Lieutenant
Do	Edward C. Euston	Do	Mar. 26, 1865,	
Company B:				
Captain	Levi Weise	Berks	Dec. 18, 1864,	
First Lieutenant	Daniel H. Pyle		Dec. 18, 1864,	
Company C:				
Captain	Reuben Snavely	Lebanon	Dec. 11, 1864,	
First Lieutenant	Reuben Snavely	Do	Oct. 29, 1864,	To Captain
Do	Edwin W. Stoner	Do	Dec. 11, 1864,	
Second Lieutenant	William Risser	Do	Dec. 11, 1864,	
Company D:				
Second Lieutenant	Peter Fisher		May 3, 1865,	
Company E:				
First Lieutenant	Franklin Philipi	Somerset	Nov. 15, 1864,	Hon. discharged, to date June 13, 1865

NINETY-THIRD REGIMENT—Continued.

RANK.	NAME.	CO. OF RESIDENCE.	DATE OF RANK.	REMARKS.
First Lieutenant....	David E. Beistel........	Dauphin........	June 13, 1865,	
Second Lieutenant..	David E. Beistel........	....Do	Nov. 15, 1864,	To First Lieutenant ....
Company F:				
Second Lieutenant..	Michael Shaeffer........	Lebanon	May 7, 1864,	
Company G:				
Captain..............	A. F. Kuhn..............	Somerset........	Nov. 26, 1864,	Not mustered ....
Do	John R. Kuhn............	....Do	Mar. 11, 1865,	
First Lieutenant	John R. Kuhn............	....Do	Nov. 26, 1864,	To Captain.........
Second Lieutenant..	Daniel B. Zimmerman..	....Do	Nov. 26, 1864,	
Company H:				
Second Lieutenant..	Jared Runyan	Columbia.........	June 15, 1864,	Hon. discharged, to date May 15, 1865...
Do	Frederic Laubach.......		May 15, 1865,	
Company I:				
Captain..............	Henry Schwartz	Lebanon	Sept. 27, 1864,	
First Lieutenant....	Calvin Umberger.......	Dauphin.........	Sept. 27, 1864,	
Second Lieutenant..	John H. Parthemer		Sept. 27, 1864,	

EXECUTIVE MILITARY DEPARTMENT. 107

OFFICERS OF THE 95th REGIMENT, INFANTRY.

RANK.	NAME.	CO. OF RESIDENCE.	DATE OF RANK.	REMARKS.
Colonel...............	John Harper...............	Philadelphia......	April 3, 1865,	
Lieutenant Colonel.	John Harper...............	......Do............	Nov. 3, 1864,	To Colonel...............
Do	John A. Ward............	......Do............	April 3, 1865,	
Major..................	John A. Ward............	......Do............	Nov. 3, 1864,	To Lieutenant Colonel......
Do	Wm. J. MacDonald......	......Do............	April 3, 1865,	
Company A:				
Captain...............	James J. Carroll.........	Philadelphia......	Dec. 7, 1864,	
Do	Joseph Vickery...........	......Do............	April 7, 1865,	
First Lieutenant....	James S Day..............	......Do............	April 22, 1865,	
Second Lieutenant..	William J. Stivers.......	......Do............	Dec. 7, 1864,	Discharged............
Do	James S. Day..............	......Do............	April 7, 1865,	To First Lieutenant.
Company B:				
First Lieutenant....	Thomas M. Field.........	Philadelphia......	April 20, 1865,	
Second Lieutenant..	Thomas M. Field.........	......Do............	Dec. 7, 1864,	To First Lieutenant..
Do	John B. Thompson......	......Do............	April 20, 1865,	
Company C:				
Captain............ ...	Marshall C. Hong........	Philadelphia......	Dec. 7, 1864,	
First Lieutenant....	Alexander H. Fry.......	......Do............	Dec. 7, 1864,	
Second Lieutenant..	John Southwell...........	......Do............	Dec. 7, 1864,	
Do	Michael Lawn	......Do............	April 20, 1865,	
Company D:				
Captain...............	David Gorden.............	Philadelphia......	Nov. 3, 1864,	
First Lieutenant....	William J. Logan	......Do............	Nov. 3, 1864,	

108　　　　　　　　　　ANNUAL REPORT OF THE

NINETY-FIFTH REGIMENT—Continued.

RANK.	NAME.	CO. OF RESIDENCE.	DATE OF RANK.	REMARKS.
Second Lieutenant..	William J. Logan......	Philadelphia.....	Dec. 7, 1864,	To First Lieutenant.......
Do	Conrad Miller......	......Do	Nov. 3, 1864,	
Company E:				
Captain.........	John M. Hughes.........	Philadelphia.....	May 16, 1865,	
First Lieutenant	John M. Hughes..........	......Do	May 20, 1865,	To Captain.........
Second Lieutenant..	Philip W. Cool...........	......Do	May 20, 1865,	
Company F:				
Captain.........	Thomas P. Smith.......	Philadelphia.....	Mar. 21, 1865,	
First Lieutenant	Samuel Johnson	..... Do	Mar. 21, 1865,	
Second Lieutenant..	Henry L. Esrey	......Do	Mar. 21, 1865,	
Company G:				
Captain.........	James M. Treichler.....	Montgomery......	Feb. 11, 1865,	
First Lieutenant	John Williams	Dauphin..........	Feb. 11, 1865,	
Second Lieutenant..	Jonathan C. Bear	Philadelphia.....	Apr. 15, 1865,	
Company H:				
Captain.........	John S. Carpenter.......	Philadelphia.....	April 20, 1865,	
First Lieutenant.....	John Southwell..........	......Do	April 20, 1865,	
Company I:				
Captain.........	Jacob C. Schuler........	Philadelphia.....	April 13, 1865,	
First Lieutenant.....	William Sharpley	......Do	April 13, 1865,	
Second Lieutenant..	Samuel O. Rutter........	......Do	April 13, 1865,	

OFFICERS OF THE 97th REGIMENT, INFANTRY.

RANK.	NAME.	CO. OF RESIDENCE.	DATE OF RANK.	REMARKS.
Colonel...............	John Wainwright.......	Chester.......	June 1, 1865,	....
Lieutenant Colonel.	John Wainwright.......	....Do.......	Jan. 15, 1865,	To Colonel............
Do...............	William H. Martin.....	Lancaster.......	June 1, 1865,	....
Major...............	William H. Martin.....	....Do.......	Jan. 15, 1865,	To Lieutenant Colonel...
Do...............	Leonard R. Thomas....	Chester.......	June 1, 1865,	....
Adjutant............	Elwood P. Baldwin....	....Do.......	May 1, 1865,	....
Quartermaster......	George L. Taggart.....	....Do.......	Jan. 1, 1865,	....
Do...............	John H. Brower........	....Do.......	May 1, 1865,	....
Company A:				
Captain............	Lewis E. Hampton.....	Chester.......	Feb. 28, 1865,	....
Do...............	Robert L. Black.......	....Do.......	June 15, 1865,	....
First Lieutenant...	Robert L. Black.......	....Do.......	Feb. 28, 1865,	To Captain............
Do...............	Frank C. Henry........	....Do.......	June 15, 1865,	....
Second Lieutenant.	Frank C. Henry........	....Do.......	May 1, 1865,	To First Lieutenant......
Do...............	Joseph Phillips........	....Do.......	June 15, 1865,	....
Company B:				
Captain............	Dallas Crow...........	Chester.......	Feb. 1, 1865,	....
First Lieutenant...	David S. Harry........	....Do.......	Feb. 1, 1865,	....
Second Lieutenant.	John B. Griffith.......	....Do.......	May 1, 1865,	....
Company C:				
Captain............	Leonard R. Thomas....	Chester.......	Feb. 1, 1865,	To Major............
Do...............	George W. Abel........	....Do.......	June 1, 1865,	....
First Lieutenant...	George W. Abel........	....Do.......	Feb. 1, 1865,	To Captain............
Do...............	Charles Warren........	....Do.......	June 1, 1865,	....

NINETY-SEVENTH REGIMENT—Continued.

RANK.	NAME.	CO. OF RESIDENCE.	DATE OF RANK.	REMARKS.
Second Lieutenant.	Charles Warren	Chester	May 1, 1865,	To First Lieutenant
Do	Cyrus B. Showalter	Do	June 1, 1865,	
Company D:				
Captain	Isaac B. Taylor	Delaware	Feb. 15, 1865,	
First Lieutenant	David W. Odiorne	Do	Feb. 15, 1865,	
Second Lieutenant.	John W. Brooks	Chester	Feb. 15, 1865,	
Company E:				
Captain	Samuel D. Smith	Chester	May 1, 1865,	
First Lieutenant	John C. Nicholson	Do	May 1, 1865,	
Second Lieutenant.	John Sullivan	Do	May 1, 1865,	
Company F:				
Captain	Lewis P. Malin	Chester	Feb. 28, 1865,	
First Lieutenant	Isaac J. Nichols	Do	Feb. 28, 1865,	
Second Lieutenant.	John E. Huntsman	Do	May 1, 1865,	
Company G:				
Captain	Washington W. James	Delaware	May 1, 1865,	
First Lieutenant	Josiah Bird	Do	May 1, 1865,	
Second Lieutenant.	Jeremiah Yoast	Do	May 1, 1865,	
Company H:				
Second Lieutenant.	Isaac L. Dutton	Chester	May 1, 1865,	

Company K:

Captain	Wm. S. Underwood	Chester	Feb. 28, 1865,
First Lieutenant	Wm. M. Sullivan	Do	Feb. 28, 1865,
Second Lieutenant	Marriott Brosius	Do	Feb. 28, 1865,
Do	John W. Thompson	Do	May 1, 1865,

OFFICERS OF THE 98th REGIMENT, INFANTRY.

RANK.	NAME.	CO. OF RESIDENCE.	DATE OF RANK.	REMARKS.
Lieutenant Colonel..	Charles Reen............	Philadelphia.....	Jan. 21, 1865,	....
Major.....................	Bernhard Gessler.......	Do	June 1, 1865,	....
Quartermaster........	Gustav Sahling	Do	Oct. 3, 1864,	....
Company A:				
First Lieutenant....	Enos Stratton...........	Philadelphia.....	Feb. 1, 1865,	....
Second Lieutenant..	Peter Adams..............	Do	June 1, 1865,	....
Company B:				
Captain.................	Frederick Muesse.......	Philadelphia.....	Oct. 3, 1864,	....
Do	Julius Damreau..........	Do	June 8, 1865,	....
First Lieutenant....	Julius Damreau..........	Do	Oct. 3, 1864,	To Captain.
Do	Gustav Futterknecht....	Do	June 8, 1865,	....
Company C:				
Captain.................	John Reese...............	Philadelphia.....	Dec. 6, 1864,	....
First Lieutenant....	William Grimm...........	Do	Dec. 23, 1864,	....
Second Lieutenant..	Andreas King............	Do	June 1, 1865,	....
Company D:				
Captain.................	John Linder..............	Philadelphia.....	June 1, 1865,	....
First Lieutenant....	Frederick Otto..........	Do	June 1, 1865,	....
Second Lieutenant..	Aug. Mosbach.............	Do	June 1, 1865,	....
Company E:				
Captain.................	Frank Beeker.............	Philadelphia.....	Dec. 6, 1864,	....
First Lieutenant....	Charles Huckel..........	Do	Feb. 1, 1865,	....

EXECUTIVE MILITARY DEPARTMENT. 113

Company F:				
Captain	Peter Fallenstein	Philadelphia	June 1, 1865,	
First Lieutenant	Hugh Armstrong	Do	June 1, 1865,	
Second Lieutenant	John Bart	Do	June 1, 1865,	
Company G:				
Captain	Leopold Herzig	Philadelphia	June 1, 1865,	
First Lieutenant	John Ambacher	Do	June 1, 1865,	
Second Lieutenant	Frederick Renner	Do	June 1, 1865,	
Company H:				
Captain	John Nava	Philadelphia	Feb. 1, 1865,	
Do	William Fratz	Do	June 1, 1865,	
First Lieutenant	William Fratz	Do	Feb. 1, 1865,	To Captain
Do	Aug. Gehrke	Do	June 1, 1865,	
Second Lieutenant	John Ruehl	Do	June 1, 1865,	
Company I:				
Captain	Jacob Schmid	Philadelphia	June 1, 1865,	
First Lieutenant	Herman Solbrig	Do	Dec. 6, 1864,	
Do	John Hirschling	Do	June 1, 1865,	
Second Lieutenant	Adolph Uhl	Do	June 1, 1865,	
Company K:				
First Lieutenant	Henry Orgs	Philadelphia	Sept. 14, 1864,	
Second Lieutenant	William Bayer	Do	June 1, 1865,	

8 MILITARY DEPART.

OFFICERS OF THE 89th REGIMENT, INFANTRY.

RANK.	NAME.	CO. OF RESIDENCE	DATE OF RANK.	REMARKS.
Company A:				
First Lieutenant...	Chas. H. Fasnacht.....	Philadelphia.....	Jan. 27, 1865,	....
Company B:				
First Lieutenant....	Frederick Klein..........	Philadelphia.....	Aug. 21, 1864,	Died April 20, 1865.
Do	Amos Cramer	Lancaster.........	April 21, 1865,	....
Second Lieutenant.	Amos Cramer	......Do	Aug. 21, 1864,	To First Lieutenant.....
Do.................	John Arrison	Philadelphia.....	April 21, 1865,	....
Company C:				
Captain...........	Harvey M. Munsell......	Venango	Sept. 12, 1864,	....
First Lieutenant....	Benjamin F Groff.......	Philadelphia.....	Sept. 12, 1864,	....
Second Lieutenant.	George W. Rogan........	......Do	Sept. 12, 1864,	....
Company E:				
Second Lieutenant.	Adam Potts..............	Philadelphia.....	Jan. 17, 1865,	....
Company F:				
First Lieutenant....	William H. Phillips.....	Philadelphia.....	Sept. 12, 1864,	....
Second Lieutenant.	William H Phillips......	......Do	Sept. 12, 1864,	....
Do	James P. Wheatleigh.....	......Do	Sept. 12, 1864,	To First Lieutenant.....
Company G:				
Captain...............	Sylvester Bonnaffon	Philadelphia.....	Sept. 21, 1864,	....
First Lieutenant.....	William A. Kite	......Do	Sept. 21, 1864,	....
Second Lieutenant..	Hugh O'Neal...........	......Do	Sept. 21, 1864,	....

EXECUTIVE MILITARY DEPARTMENT.

Second Lieutenant..	John Witmire............	Philadelphia......	Jan. 13, 1865,
Company I; Second Lieutenant..	John Davis...............	Philadelphia......	Oct. 8, 1864,

OFFICERS OF THE 100th REGIMENT, INFANTRY.

RANK.	NAME.	CO. OF RESIDENCE.	DATE OF RANK.	REMARKS.
Colonel...............	Norman J. Maxwell....	Mercer............	April 8, 1865,	....
Lieutenant Colonel.	Charles Wilson..........	Lawrence.........	April 8, 1865,	....
Major..................	James W. Bard..........	Allegheny........	April 8, 1865,	....
Quartermaster.......	Richard D. Holmes.....	......Do............	Feb. 1, 1865,	....
Company A :				
Captain...............	John H. Atkinson.......	Allegheny........	Mar. 8, 1865,	....
First Lieutenant....	John H. Atkinson.......	......Do............	Jan. 11, 1865,	To Captain......
Do....................	William H. Billings....	Washington......	Mar. 8, 1865,	To First Lieutenant......
Second Lieutenant..	William H. Billings.....	......Do............	Feb. 23, 1865,	....
Do....................	George M. Metzner.....	......Do............	Mar. 8, 1865,	....
Company B :				
Second Lieutenant..	William M. Gibson.....	Lawrence.........	Feb. 25, 1865,	....
Company C :				
Second Lieutenant..	William Smiley..........	Lawrence.........	Mar. 13, 1865,	....
Company D :				
Captain...............	John L. Johnston.......	Beaver............	Dec. 13, 1864,	....
First Lieutenant....	John C. Harb............	....Do..............	Dec. 13, 1864,	....
Second Lieutenant..	Robert J. Douthill......	....Do..............	Feb. 25, 1865,	....
Company E :				
Captain...............	David P. Book...........	Lawrence.........	Oct. 26, 1864,	....
First Lieutenant....	John Bentley.............	....Do..............	Oct. 26, 1864,	....
Second Lieutenant..	William H. Corbin......	....Do..............	Feb. 25, 1865,	....

EXECUTIVE MILITARY DEPARTMENT. 117

Company F:				
Second Lieutenant..	Thomas Arrow.........	Lawrence.........	Mar. 13, 1865,	....
Company G:				
Second Lieutenant..	Robert P. Douglass.....	Lawrence.........	Mar. 13, 1865,	....
Company H:				
Captain.............	Isaac S. Pyle............	Lawrence.........	Mar. 8, 1865,	....
First Lieutenant....	Isaac S. Pyle............	.......Do.........	Oct. 26, 1864,	To Captain........
Do.............	Robert G. Christy........	.......Do.........	Mar. 8, 1865,	....
Second Lieutenant..	Robert G. Christy........	.......Do.........	Mar. 13, 1865,	To First Lieutenant.
Do.............	Hillery W. Bay..........	.......Do.........	Mar. 8, 1865,	....
Company K:				
First Lieutenant....	John H. Stevenson......	Lawrence.........	April 26, 1865,	....
Second Lieutenant..	John H. Stevenson......	.......Do.........	Mar. 13, 1865,	To First Lieutenant.
Do.............	Samuel M. Dickson......	.......Do.........	April 26, 1865,	....
Company M:				
First Lieutenant....	Charles Oliver..........	Allegheny........	Mar. 15, 1865,	....
Second Lieutenant..	William Oliver..........	.......Do.........	Mar. 15, 1865,	....

OFFICERS OF THE 101st REGIMENT, INFANTRY.

RANK.	NAME.	CO. OF RESIDENCE.	DATE OF RANK.	REMARKS.
Colonel............	James Sheafer............	Cumberland......	May 18, 1865,	....
Lieutenant Colonel.	Melvin L. Clark..........	Tioga.............	May 18, 1865,	....
Major.............	David W. Mullin.........	Bedford..........	May 18, 1865,	....
Do	Henry S. Benner.........	Adams............	June 1, 1865,	....
Adjutant..........	Thomas Bushman.......	....	May 18, 1865,	....
Quartermaster......	David M. Ramsey.......	Beaver............	May 18, 1865,	To Captain Company F......
Company A:				
Captain............	Edgar Lee...............	Cumberland	May 18, 1865,	....
First lieutenant....	Henry M. Johnston.....	....	May 18, 1865,	....
Second Lieutenant.	James Gilmore..........	....	May 18, 1865,	....
Company B:				
Captain............	Dyer J. Butts.............	Tioga.............	June 1, 1865,	....
First Lieutenant....	George Hollins...........	....Do...........	June 1, 1865,	....
Second Lieutenant.	Justus B. Clark..........	....Do...........	June 1, 1865,	....
Company C:				
Captain............	Charles W. Thompson..	Lawrence.........	June 1, 1865,	....
First Lieutenant....	Joseph C. Cubbison.....	....Do...........	June 1, 1865,	....
Second Lieutenant.	Nathan Cory.............	....Do...........	June 1, 1865,	....
Company D:				
Captain............	Henry Lynn..............	Bedford..........	June 1, 1865,	....
Company E:				
Captain............	James M. Morrow......	Allegheny........	June 1, 1865,	....

EXECUTIVE MILITARY DEPARTMENT.

First Lieutenant.....	Elias B. Durbin..........	Allegheny.........	June 1, 1865.
Company F :			
Captain..............	David M Ramsey.......	Beaver.............	June 1, 1865,
First Lieutenant....	Wm. H. Sutberland	...Do	June 1, 1865,
Second Lieutenant..	Brunton W. Smith......	....Do.............	June 1, 1865,
Company G :			
Captain.............	Isaiah Conley...........	Bedford............	May 18, 1865,
First Lieutenant ...	John B. Helm............	....Do	May 18, 1865,
Second Lieutenant..	John Paul................	Allegheny.........	June 1, 1865,
Company I :			
Captain.............	John Parry...............	Schuylkill........	June 1, 1865,
First Lieutenant	Richard Morris.........	.....Do............	June 1, 1865,
Company K :			
Captain.............	Thomas H Heppard...	Philadelphia......	June 1, 1865,
First Lieutenant ...	William H. Bell.........	Adams.............	June 1, 1865,
Second Lieutenant..	Conrad Snyder..........	....Do	June 1, 1865,
Company A, 2 :			
Captain.............	Levi Musser.............	Dauphin	Mar. 14, 1865,
First Lieutenant....	Henry P. Owens.........	.....Do............	Mar. 14, 1865,
Second Lieutenant..	John T. Metlin	.....Do............	Mar. 14, 1865,
Company B, 2 :			
Captain.............	William S. Harrah......	Westmoreland ...	Mar. 16, 1865,
First Lieutenant....	Jacob D. Kettering......	.......Do	Mar. 16, 1865,
Second Lieutenant..	James M'Cauley........	........Do	Mar. 16, 1865,
Company C, 2 :			
Captain.............	William Fiethorn........	Union..............	Mar. 18, 1865,

ONE HUNDRED AND FIRST REGIMENT—Continued.

RANK.	NAME.	CO. OF RESIDENCE.	DATE OF RANK.	REMARKS.
First Lieutenant....	Samuel B. Reber.........	Union.............	Mar. 18, 1865,	
Second Lieutenant..	Hubley Albright.........	....Do.............	Mar. 18, 1865,	
Company D, 2:				
Captain................	Marshall Winebrenner..	Dauphin.........	Mar. 22, 1865,	
First Lieutenant....	Reuben S. Reed..........	....Do.............	Mar. 22, 1865,	
Second Lieutenant..	Daniel Winters...........	....Do.............	Mar. 22, 1865,	
Company E, 2:				
Captain................	Cornelius M'Clellan.....	Juniata..........	Mar. 23, 1865,	
First Lieutenant....	Benjamin Geipe..........	York..............	Mar. 23, 1865,	
Second Lieutenant..	Joseph Vanormer........	Juniata..........	Mar. 23, 1865,	
Company F, 2:				
Captain................	William B. Wolf.........	Cumberland	Mar. 24, 1865,	
First Lieutenant....	John W. Mountz.........	....Do.............	Mar. 24, 1865,	
Second Lieutenant..	John Hoffert..............	....Do.............	Mar. 24, 1865,	
Do	Thomas M. Finney......	....Do.............	July 16, 1865,	Died July 15, 1865.....
Company G, 2:				
Captain................	Theodore C. Norris......	Adams............	Mar. 25, 1865,	
First Lieutenant....	Robert George...........	Allegheny......	Mar. 25, 1865,	
Second Lieutenant..	Samuel A. Young........	Adams............	Mar. 25, 1865,	
Company H, 2:				
Captain................	Henry W. Larimer......	Allegheny......	Mar. 27, 1865,	
First Lieutenant....	Bradley D. Salter........	....Do.............	Mar. 27, 1865,	
Second Lieutenant..	Hugh M. Hall.............	....Do.............	Mar. 27, 1865,	

EXECUTIVE MILITARY DEPARTMENT. 121

OFFICERS OF THE 102d REGIMENT, INFANTRY.

RANK.	NAME.	CO. OF RESIDENCE.	DATE OF RANK.	REMARKS.
Colonel	James Patchell	Allegheny	April 18, 1865,	
Lieutenant Colonel	James D. Kirk	Do	April 18, 1865,	
Do	James D. Duncan	Do	June 23, 1865,	
Major	James D. Duncan	Do	April 18, 1865,	To Lieutenant Colonel.
Do	Robert W. Lyon	Butler	June 23, 1865,	
Adjutant	George W. Harper	Allegheny	June 25, 1865,	
Chaplain	David Jones	Beaver	Mar. 27, 1865,	
Company A:				
Second Lieutenant	Wm. G. Greenawalt	Allegheny	May 5, 1865,	
Company B:				
First Lieutenant	Presley J. Brown	Allegheny	June 17, 1865,	
Second Lieutenant	John G. Williams	Do	June 17, 1865,	
Company C:				
First Lieutenant	John P. Megogney	Allegheny	June 25, 1865,	
Second Lieutenant	William M. Whitaker	Do	June 25, 1865,	
Company D:				
Captain	Augustus Myers	Allegheny	June 17, 1865,	
First Lieutenant	William H. Ballard	Do	June 17, 1865,	
Second Lieutenant	William H. Ballard	Do	May 5, 1865,	To First Lieutenant.
Do	Alonzo Sterling	Do	June 25, 1865,	
Company E:				
Second Lieutenant	William B. Sands	Allegheny	May 5, 1865,	

ANNUAL REPORT OF THE

ONE HUNDRED AND SECOND REGIMENT—Continued.

RANK.	NAME.	CO. OF RESIDENCE.	DATE OF RANK	REMARKS.
Company F:				
Captain............	Hugh M'Ilvaine............	Allegheny........	April 18, 1865,	....
First Lieutenant....	Marcus Barker............	Do	April 18, 1865,	....
Do............	Benj F. M'Gowan........	Do	June 25, 1865,	....
Second Lieutenant.	Benj F. M'Gowan........	Do	April 18, 1865,	To First Lieutenant......
Do	William Jones	Do	June 25, 1865,	....
Company G:				
Second Lieutenant.	David Hunter.............	Allegheny........	May 5, 1865,	....
Company H:				
Captain	Isaac C. Stewart.........	Butler	June 25, 1865,	....
First Lieutenant....	Isaac C. Stewart.........	Do	June 17, 1865,	To Captain........
Do............	John Koltoubaugh........	Do	June 25, 1865,	....
Second Lieutenant.	Eli Conn	Do	June 25, 1865,	....
Company I:				
Captain............	George W. Gillespie....	Allegheny........	June 17, 1865,	....
First Lieutenant....	William H. Ayers. ...	Butler	June 25, 1865,	....
Second Lieutenant.	George W. Gillespie.....	Allegheny........	May 5, 1865,	To Captain.........
Do............	Archibald D. Thompson,	Do	June 25, 1865,	....
Company K:				
Second Lieutenant.	James Harsher............	Allegheny........	June 25, 1865,	....
Company L:				
Captain............	Isaac Coldran.............	Allegheny........	June 25, 1865,	....

EXECUTIVE MILITARY DEPARTMENT. 123

First Lieutenant.....	Isaac Coldran........	Allegheny........	May 5, 1865,	To Captain.........
Second Lieutenant..	Theodore F. Sheering...	Do...............	June 25, 1865,	....
Do	Robert D. Duncan.......	Do...............	June 25, 1865,	....
Company M :				
Captain.............	John Aiken...........	Allegheny........	June 17, 1865,	....
First Lieutenant....	Albert Anderson......	Do...............	June 17, 1865,	....
Second Lieutenant...	Albert Anderson......	Do...............	May 5, 1865,	To First Lieutenant...
Do	John E. Williams	Do...............	June 25, 1865,	....

ANNUAL REPORT OF THE

OFFICERS OF THE 103d REGIMENT, INFANTRY.

RANK.	NAME.	CO. OF RESIDENCE.	DATE OF RANK.	REMARKS.
Company A, 2:				
Captain...............	E. K. Lehman......	Franklin...........	Mar. 16, 1865,	
First Lieutenant....	George C. Carson.....	Adams.......	Mar. 17, 1865,	
Second Lieutenant..	Samuel H. Eicholtz....	...Do........	Mar. 17, 1865,	
Company B, 2:				
Captain...............	George H. Jones......	Lycoming......	Mar. 28, 1865,	
First Lieutenant....	Elias B. Yordy.........	Columbia......	Mar. 28, 1865,	
Second Lieutenant..	William E. Sterner.....	......Do........	Mar. 28, 1865,	
Company C, 2:				
Captain........	George Shipp.........	Northumberland,	Mar. 29, 1865,	
First Lieutenant....	Jefferson M. John......	......Do.......	Mar. 29, 1865,	
Second Lieutenant..	Owen M. Fowler......	......Do.......	Mar. 29, 1865,	
Company D, 2:				
Captain...............	Emanuel Herman......	York........	Mar. 30, 1865,	
First Lieutenant....	Edmund Rutter........	...Do........	Mar. 31, 1865,	
Second Lieutenant..	Charles W. P. Collins..	...Do........	Mar. 31, 1865,	
Company E, 2:				
Captain...............	De Los Walker.......	Crawford......	April 3, 1865,	
First Lieutenant....	A. J. Walker...........	...Do........	April 3, 1865,	
Second Lieutenant..	A. S. Bates...........	...Do........	April 3, 1865,	
Company F, 2:				
Captain...............	Cyrus Thomas.........	Westmoreland...	April 5, 1865,	

First Lieutenant.....	Caleb M. Row........	Westmoreland...	April 5, 1865,
Second Lieutenant..	Solomon A. Bryan.....	........Do...........	April 5, 1865,
Company G, 2:			
Captain.............	Cornelius A. Harper....	Dauphin	April 12, 1865,
First Lieutenant.....	Samuel S. Matthews....	York............	April 12, 1865,
Second Lieutenant..	Daniel Y. Lenker	Dauphin	April 12, 1865,
Company H, 2:			
Captain.............	John W. Dougherty....	Blair...........	April 12, 1865,
First Lieutenant	Joseph D. Davis........	Indiana.........	April 12, 1865,
Second Lieutenant..	Robert Carson.........	......Do	April 18, 1865,

OFFICERS OF THE 104th REGIMENT, INFANTRY.

RANK.	NAME.	CO. OF RESIDENCE.	DATE OF RANK.	REMARKS.
Colonel	Theophilus Kephart	Bucks	Apr. 1, 1865,	
Lieutenant Colonel	Theophilus Kephart	Do	Feb. 24, 1865,	To Colonel
Do	John M'D. Laughlin	Do	Apr. 1, 1865,	
Major	Theophilus Kephart	Do	Nov. 21, 1864,	To Lieutenant Colonel
Do	John M'D. Laughlin	Do	Feb. 24, 1865,	To Lieutenant Colonel
Do	Thos. B. Scarborough	Do	Apr. 1, 1865,	
Adjutant	Henry A. Widdifield	Do	Feb. 24, 1865,	
Company A:				
Captain	George S. Conner	Bucks	Feb. 24, 1865,	
First Lieutenant	George S. Conner	Do	Nov. 21, 1864,	To Captain
Do	John J. Wigton	Do	Feb. 24, 1865,	
Second Lieutenant	John J. Wigton	Do	Nov. 21, 1864,	To First Lieutenant
Do	Andrew J. Terry	Do	Feb. 24, 1865,	
Company B:				
Captain	Jacob W. Glase	Bucks	Nov. 21, 1864,	
First Lieutenant	Henry A. Widdifield	Do	Nov. 21, 1864,	To Adjutant
Do	John Dyer	Do	Feb. 24, 1865,	
Second Lieutenant	John Dyer	Do	Nov. 21, 1864,	To First Lieutenant
Do	John C. Nelson	Do	Feb. 24, 1865,	
Company C:				
Captain	Charles T. Michener	Bucks	Apr. 1, 1865,	
First Lieutenant	Charles T. Michener	Do	Nov. 29, 1864,	To Captain
Do	Nathaniel Gamble	Do	Apr. 1, 1865,	
Second Lieutenant	Nathaniel Gamble	Do	Feb. 24, 1865,	To First Lieutenant
Do	Seneca Beal	Do	Apr. 1, 1865,	

EXECUTIVE MILITARY DEPARTMENT. 127

Company D:				
Captain............	Samuel N. Garren........	Bucks........	Apr. 1, 1865,	....
First Lieutenant....	Samuel N. Garren........	....Do	Nov. 29, 1864,	To Captain...
Company E:				
Captain............	Robert Johnson..........	Blair........	Feb. 24, 1865,	....
First Lieutenant....	John H. Keatley.........	....Do	Feb. 24, 1865,	....
Second Lieutenant...	William Rodamer.........	....Do	Feb. 24, 1865,	....
Company F:				
Captain............	Joel F. Frederick........	....	Mar. 23, 1865,	....
First Lieutenant	David C. Orvis	....	Mar. 23, 1865,	....
Second Lieutenant...	William Flickinger.......	....	Mar. 23, 1865,	....
Company G:				
Captain............	John W. Kantner........	Schuylkill....	Mar. 21, 1865,	....
First Lieutenant ...	William A. Christian.....	....Do	Mar. 21, 1865,	....
Second Lieutenant...	Elius Sassaman	....Do	Mar. 21, 1865,	....
Company H:				
First Lieutenant....	William J. Walker.......	Bucks........	Oct. 27, 1864,	....
Second Lieutenant...	Joel Setley	....Do	Oct. 27, 1864,	....
Company I:				
Captain............	William H. Rankin.......	Luzerne......	Mar. 28, 1865,	....
First Lieutenant....	Frank W. Watson........	....Do	Mar. 28, 1865,	....
Do	John W. Barnes.........	....Do	June 21, 1865,	....
Second Lieutenant...	John W. Barnes.........	....Do	Mar. 28, 1865,	To First Lieutenant
Do	John F. Montague.......	Montour......	June 21, 1865,	....
Company K:				
Captain............	Martin M'Canna........	Armstrong ...	Mar. 17, 1865,	....
First Lieutenant....	Joel Crawford...........	....Do	Mar. 17, 1865,	....
Second Lieutenant...	Samuel A. Browser......	....Do	Mar. 17, 1865,	....

OFFICERS OF THE 105th REGIMENT, INFANTRY.

RANK.	NAME.	CO. OF RESIDENCE.	DATE OF RANK.	REMARKS.
Colonel	James Miller	Jefferson	April 25, 1865,	
Lieutenant Colonel	Oliver C. Redic	Butler	April 25, 1865,	To Colonel.
Major	James Miller	Jefferson	Oct. 28, 1864,	
Company A:				
Captain	John H. M'Kee	Jefferson	Oct. 5, 1864,	
First Lieutenant	James W. Washob	Do	Oct. 5, 1864,	To First Lieutenant.
Second Lieutenant	James W. Washob	Do	Dec. 13, 1864,	
Do	William M. Blose	Do	Oct. 5, 1864,	
Company B:				
Captain	Joseph C. Kelso	Jefferson	Nov. 28, 1864,	
First Lieutenant	William N. Pearse	Franklin	Nov. 28, 1864,	
Do	John A. M'Lain	Jefferson	Nov. 28, 1864,	
Second Lieutenant	J. J. Parsons	Do	Nov. 28, 1864,	
Company C:				
First Lieutenant	R. G. Warden	Beaver	Mar. 20, 1865,	
Second Lieutenant	H. H. Michaels	Clearfield	Mar. 20, 1865,	
Company D:				
First Lieutenant	Joseph L. Evans	Allegheny	Mar. 16, 1865,	
Second Lieutenant	George Gibson	Do	Mar. 16, 1865,	
Company F:				
Second Lieutenant	Ogg Neil	Indiana	Oct. 10, 1864,	

EXECUTIVE MILITARY DEPARTMENT.

Captain	Jacob H. Freas	Jefferson	Dec. 13, 1864,	
First Lieutenant	Benjamin W. Stauffer	Do	Dec. 13, 1864,	
Second Lieutenant	E. P. Shaw	Do	Dec. 18, 1864,	
Company I:				
Captain	Henry Galbraith	Jefferson	April 25, 1865,	
First Lieutenant	John H. West	Allegheny	April 25, 1865,	
Second Lieutenant	J. H. Kennedy	Jefferson	April 25, 1865,	
Company K:				
Captain	Milton W. Adair	Indiana	Oct. 28, 1864,	
First Lieutenant	John M. Bruce	Do	Oct. 28, 1864,	
Second Lieutenant	John Gold	Jefferson	April 25, 1865,	

9 MILITARY DEPART.

OFFICERS OF THE 106th REGIMENT, INFANTRY.

RANK.	NAME.	CO. OF RESIDENCE.	DATE OF RANK.	REMARKS.
Colonel	John H. Gallager	Philadelphia	June 23, 1865	
Lieutenant Colonel	John H. Gallager	Do	May 27, 1865	To Colonel.
Do	Francis Wessels	Do	June 23, 1865	
Major	Ralph B. Clark	Do	June 23, 1865	
Adjutant	Ralph B. Clark	Do	Oct. 1, 1864	To Major.
Do	Richard F. Whitmoyer	Columbia	June 23, 1865	
Company F:				
Captain	Charles M'Coy	Philadelphia	June 8, 1865	
Second Lieutenant	Charles H. Weinert	Do	June 8, 1865	
Company H:				
Captain	James C. Reynolds	Philadelphia	June 23, 1865	
First Lieutenant	William B. Rose	Do	Jan. 4, 1865	Mustered out.
Do	Charles M'Coy	Do	April 22, 1865	To Captain Company F.
Do	James C. Reynolds	Do	June 8, 1865	To Captain.
Second Lieutenant	Frederick Weiderman	Do	June 23, 1865	
	Frederick Weiderman	Do	June 8, 1865	To First Lieutenant.
Company K:				
Captain	John H. Gallager	Philadelphia	Jan. 13, 1865	To Lieutenant Colonel.
Do	Edward J. Lathrop	Do	June 8, 1865	
First Lieutenant	Edward J. Lathrop	Do	Oct. 1, 1864	To Captain.
Do	Charles Rettew	Do	June 8, 1865	
Second Lieutenant	William E. Wagner	Do	June 8, 1865	

EXECUTIVE MILITARY DEPARTMENT. 131

OFFICERS OF THE 107th REGIMENT, INFANTRY.

RANK.	NAME.	CO. OF RESIDENCE.	DATE OF RANK.	REMARKS.
Major.............	Edwin E. Zeigler........	Mifflin............	Mar. 8, 1865,	....
Quartermaster........	John M. Montgomery...	Franklin..........	Mar. 12, 1865,	....
Company A:				
Captain.............	Oliver P. Stair..........	York.............	Feb. 22, 1865,	....
Do..............	Samuel Lyon...........	Fulton...........	June 3, 1865,	....
First Lieutenant......	James Crimmins........	York.............	July 7, 1865,	....
Second Lieutenant....	James Crimmins........	Do...............	June 3, 1865,	To First Lieutenant........
Do...............	Peter A. Hinkle........	Monroe...........	July 7, 1865,	....
Company B:				
Captain.............	William R. Sturgeon....	Cumberland.......	Jan. 12, 1865,	....
First Lieutenant......	Aaron Freher...........	Franklin..........	Jan. 12, 1865,	....
Second Lieutenant....	Aaron Freher...........	Do...............	Nov. 29, 1864,	To First Lieutenant........
Do...............	George Smith...........	Do...............	Jan. 12, 1865,	....
Company C:				
Captain.............	William Shuler..........	Montgomery......	May 15, 1865,	....
First Lieutenant......	Lord B. Green..........	Luzerne...........	May 15, 1865,	....
Second Lieutenant....	Lord B. Green..........	Do...............	Dec. 29, 1864,	To First Lieutenant........
Do...............	Thomas Wheeler........	Do...............	May 15, 1865,	....
Company D:				
Captain.............	A. W. Norris...........	Mifflin............	Mar. 19, 1865,	....
First Lieutenant......	Michael J. Hawley......	Luzerne...........	Mar. 19, 1865,	....
Second Lieutenant....	John A. Tompkins......	Do...............	Jan. 14, 1865,	To First Lieutenant Company F....
Do...............	Michael J. Hawley......	Do...............	Mar. 6, 1865,	To First Lieutenant........

ONE HUNDRED AND SEVENTH REGIMENT—Continued.

RANK.	NAME.	CO. OF RESIDENCE.	DATE OF RANK.	REMARKS.
Company E:				
Captain	Henry W. Smyser	Lancaster	Mar. 8, 1865,	
First Lieutenant	Abraham Cassel	Do	Oct. 6, 1864,	
Do	Henry W. Snyser	Do	Feb. 3, 1865,	To Captain
Second Lieutenant	Henry W. Smyser	Do	Oct. 6, 1864,	To First Lieutenant
Do	Martin V. Cochran	Do	Feb. 3, 1865,	
Company F:				
Captain	John A. Tompkins	Luzerne	Mar. 8, 1865,	
First Lieutenant	John A. Tompkins	Do	Mar. 6, 1865,	To Captain
Do	Frank H. Wentz	Mifflin	Mar. 8, 1865,	
Company G:				
Captain	James B. Thomas	Philadelphia	Mar. 8, 1865,	
First Lieutenant	James A Wattson	Franklin	April 23, 1865,	
Second Lieutenant	Edwin S. Wilcox	Do	April 23, 1865,	
Company H:				
First Lieutenant	William C. Beck	Allegheny	Mar. 9, 1865,	To Captain Company K
Second Lieutenant	John M. Montgomery	Franklin	Dec. 29, 1864,	To Quartermaster
Do	William C. Beck	Allegheny	Mar. 12, 1865,	To First Lieutenant
Company I:				
First Lieutenant	Isaac S. Dissinger	Lebanon	April 23, 1865,	
Do	John Delaney	Luzerne	July 7, 1865,	
Second Lieutenant	Isaac S. Dissinger	Lebanon	Mar. 2, 1865,	To First Lieutenant
Do	John Delaney	Luzerne	April 23, 1865,	To First Lieutenant

Company K:			
Captain............	William C. Beck............	Allegheny.........	July 7, 1865,
Second Lieutenant..	Harrison H. Hutton.....	Franklin..........	Nov. 29, 1864,
Do..............	John R. Michaels........	....Do............	July 7, 1865,

OFFICERS OF THE 108th REGIMENT, ELEVENTH CAVALRY.

RANK.	NAME.	CO. OF RESIDENCE.	DATE OF RANK.	REMARKS.
Colonel	Franklin A. Stratton	Allegheny	May 10, 1865,	
Lieutenant Colonel	James A. Skelly	Cambria	May 10, 1865,	
Major	James E. M'Farland	Chester	Feb. 17, 1865,	
Do	Robert S. Monroe	Philadelphia	Mar. 21, 1865,	
Do	John S. Nimmon	Franklin	May 10, 1865,	
Do	Archibald A. Menzies	Northampton	May 10, 1865,	
Adjutant	Samuel R. Stratton	Clarion	Jan. 27, 1865,	To Captain Company A.
Do	Jacob Samuel Weaver	Allegheny	June 9, 1865,	
Quartermaster	Furman Gulc	Wyoming	April 3, 1865,	
Commissary	James H. Clover	Clarion	Feb. 4, 1865,	
Company A:				
Captain	Samuel R. Stratton	Clarion	June 9, 1865,	
First Lieutenant	Lucius L. Carrier	Bradford	April 1, 1865,	
Second Lieutenant	Lucius L. Carrier	Do	April 4, 1865,	To First Lieutenant.
Do	Russell J. Ross	Do	April 1, 1865,	
Company B:				
Captain	John W. Ford	Chester	Feb. 17, 1865,	
First Lieutenant	Hilborn Darlington	Do	Feb. 17, 1865,	
Second Lieutenant	James M. Rigg	Philadelphia	Feb. 17, 1865,	
Company C:				
First Lieutenant	Alexander Skilton	Philadelphia	Aug. 8, 1865,	
Second Lieutenant	George S. Egerton	Do	Aug. 8, 1865,	

EXECUTIVE MILITARY DEPARTMENT.   135

Company D:				
Captain............	James E. Cook.........	Franklin......	April 1, 1865,	....
First Lieutenant....	Wm. N. Scott.........	......Do........	April 1, 1865,	....
Second Lieutenant.	Jacob W. Miles.........	......Do........	May 6, 1865,	....
Company E:				
Captain............	William Lancaster.....	Philadelphia...	Mar. 21, 1865,	....
Do............	Charles Kirkham.......	......Do.....	April 1, 1865,	To Captain......
First Lieutenant....	Charles Kirkham.......	......Do........	Mar. 21, 1865,	....
Do............	Joseph E. Bruen.......	......Do........	April 1, 1865,	....
Second Lieutenant.	Levi J. Wolfe..........	......Do........	Mar. 21, 1865,	....
Company G:				
Captain............	Robert E. Banks.......	Allegheny.....	May 10, 1865,	....
First Lieutenant....	Henry J. Hads.........	Cambria......	May 10, 1865,	....
Second Lieutenant.	Abraham Burket.......	Blair.........	May 10, 1865,	....
Company H:				
Captain............	Anthony Beers.........	Wyoming......	Feb. 13, 1865,	....
First Lieutenant....	Philip B. Moore........	Carbon........	Feb. 13, 1865,	....
Second Lieutenant.	Simeon Albee..........	....Do.........	Feb. 13, 1865,	....
Company I:				
First Lieutenant....	Frank P. Farrell.......	Lancaster.....	Dec. 9, 1864,	....
Second Lieutenant.	William Meekins.......	......Do.....	Dec. 9, 1864,	....
Company K:				
Captain............	Hiram H. White........	Luzerne.......	May 26, 1865,	....
First Lieutenant....	Hiram H. White........	....Do.....	April 3, 1865,	To Captain......
Do............	Peter W. Kreske.......	Monroe.......	May 26, 1865,	....
Second Lieutenant.	Peter W. Kreske.......	....Do.....	April 3, 1865,	To First Lieutenant...
Do............	William R. Brink......	Luzerne.......	May 26, 1865,	....

ONE HUNDRED AND EIGHTH REGIMENT—Continued.

RANK.	NAME.	CO. OF RESIDENCE.	DATE OF RANK.	REMARKS.
Company L:				
Captain............	John C. Sample.........	Franklin.........	Jan. 27, 1865,	....
Company M:				
First Lieutenant....	Jacob Samuel Weaver..	Allegheny.........	May 2, 1865,	To Adjutant........
Do	Isaac A. Smallwood.....	......Do	June 9, 1865,	....
Second Lieutenant..	Isaac A. Smallwood.....	......Do	May 2, 1865,	To First Lieutenant......
Do	Joseph W. Sylvester....	......Do	June 9, 1865,	....

OFFICERS OF THE 110th REGIMENT, INFANTRY.

RANK.	NAME.	CO. OF RESIDENCE.	DATE OF RANK.	REMARKS.
Colonel............	Franklin B. Stewart...	Blair............	June 19, 1865,	....
Lieutenant Colonel.	Isaac T. Hamilton......	...Do............	Jan. 12, 1865,	Honorably discharged as Major, to date .... [May 4, 1865.
Do	John B. Fite............	Cambria.........	May 5, 1865,	To Colonel.............
Do	Franklin B. Stewart....	Blair............	June 9, 1865,	....
Do	John L. Ellis...........	Philadelphia....	June 19, 1865,	....
Major.............	Franklin B. Stewart....	Blair............	Jan. 12, 1865,	To Lieutenant Colonel.....
Do	John L. Ellis...........	Philadelphia....	June 9, 1865,	To Lieutenant Colonel.....
Do	Samuel M'Cune.........	Blair............	June 19, 1865,	....
Adjutant..........	William H. Shelow.....	...Do............	April 18, 1865,	To Captain Company A.....
Chaplain..........	John Thomas...........	Montour	Jan. 17, 1865,	....
Company A :				
Captain...........	William H. Shelow.....	Blair............	June 19, 1865,	....
First Lieutenant...	Joseph R. Gross........	...Do............	April 18, 1865,	Not mustered...........
Do	Adam Weight...........	...Do............	April 18, 1865,	....
Second Lieutenant.	George W. Buck........	...Do............	April 18, 1865,	....
Company B :				
Captain...........	John R. Pancoast.......	Philadelphia....	Mar. 1, 1865,	....
First Lieutenant...	Enoch W. Edwards.....	Huntingdon.....	Mar. 1, 1865,	....
Second Lieutenant.	James M. Walls.........	...Do............	Mar. 1, 1865,	....
Company C :				
Captain...........	James C. Hamilton.....	Montour	Dec. 18, 1864,	....
First Lieutenant...	Samuel Kinley..........	Mifflin..........	Dec. 18, 1864,	....
Second Lieutenant.	Thomas Livingston.....	Bedford.........	Dec. 18, 1864,	....

ONE HUNDRED AND TENTH REGIMENT—Continued.

RANK.	NAME.	CO. OF RESIDENCE.	DATE OF RANK.	REMARKS.
Company D:				
Captain	Emanuel Brallier	Cambria	May 14, 1865	
Company E:				
Second Lieutenant	James G. Boileau	Philadelphia	Aug. 9, 1864	
Company F:				
Captain	Owen M'Cullin		Dec. 16, 1864	
Do	John Buckley	Philadelphia	May 19, 1865	
First Lieutenant	Andrew Cullen	Do	May 19, 1865	
Company G:				
Captain	John Dorrington	Allegheny	April 17, 1865	
First Lieutenant	David O. Brown	Westmoreland	April 17, 1865	
Second Lieutenant	William Jarvis	Allegheny	April 17, 1865	
Company H:				
Captain	Franklin B. Stewart	Blair	Dec. 3, 1864	To Major
Do	Jacob Beekhart	Philadelphia	Jan. 12, 1865	
First Lieutenant	Jacob Beekhart	Do	Dec 3, 1864	To Captain
Do	David W. Smyth	Allegheny	Jan. 12, 1865	
Second Lieutenant	John W. Davidson		Jan. 12, 1865	
Company I:				
Captain	William H. Presho	Philadelphia	June 12, 1865	
First Lieutenant	William H. Presho	Do	May 19, 1865	To Captain
Do	John Peacock	Do	June 12, 1865	

Second Lieutenant..	Thos. C. Whittingham,	Philadelphia......	June 12, 1865,
Company K:			
Captain.............	Michael Connelly........	Philadelphia......	June 13, 1865,
First Lieutenant	Patrick Desmond........	........Do...........	June 13, 1865,
Second Lieutenant..	Neal M'Laughlin.......	........Do...........	June 13, 1865,

OFFICERS OF THE 111th REGIMENT, INFANTRY.

RANK.	NAME.	CO. OF RESIDENCE.	DATE OF RANK.	REMARKS
Colonel...............	Thomas M. Walker......	Erie............	Mar. 31, 1865,	....
Lieutenant Colonel.	Wm J. Alexander......	Warren.........	April 7, 1865,	....
Do	Frank I. Osgood.........	Elk.............	May 31, 1865,	To Lieutenant Colonel.
Major.................	Wm. J. Alexander......	Warren.........	Mar. 31, 1865,	To Lieutenant Colonel.
Do	Frank I. Osgood.........	Elk.............	April 7, 1865,	....
Do	Frederick L. Gimber....	Philadelphia...	May 31, 1865,	....
Quartermaster......	Noah W. Lowell.........	Erie............	April 1, 1865,	....
Company B:				
Captain...............	John J. Haight............	Warren.........	April 1, 1865,	....
Company D:				
Captain...............	Hamilton R. Sturdevant,	Warren.........	April 7, 1865,	....
First Lieutenant....	Charles W. Culbertson,	Erie............	April 1, 1865,	....
Company I:				
First Lieutenant....	William W. Griffing.....	Philadelphia ...	April 1, 1865,	....
Company K:				
Captain...............	Plympton A. Mead.....	Elk.............	April 1, 1865,	....
First Lieutenant....	George W. Clark.........	Philadelphia...	April 1, 1865,	....

EXECUTIVE MILITARY DEPARTMENT. 141

OFFICERS OF THE 112th REGIMENT, SECOND ARTILLERY.

RANK.	NAME.	CO. OF RESIDENCE.	DATE OF RANK.	REMARKS.
Colonel	Samuel D. Strawbridge,	Montour	Mar. 8, 1865,	
Lieutenant Colonel	Samuel D. Strawbridge,	Do	Jan. 4, 1865,	To Colonel
Do	Benjamin F. Winger	Franklin	Mar. 8, 1865,	
Major	Benjamin F. Winger	Do	Jan. 4, 1865,	To Lieutenant Colonel
Do	David Schooley	Luzerne	Mar. 8, 1865,	
Do	William S. Bailey,	Philadelphia	Mar. 8, 1865,	
Company A:				
Captain	Benjamin F. Everett	Luzerne	Dec. 13, 1864,	
First Lieutenant	John G. Rick	Philadelphia	Dec. 13, 1864,	Honorably discharged, to date May 15, '65.
Second Lieutenant	John G. Rick	Do	Nov. 28, 1864,	To First Lieutenant
Do	William Mauk	Do	Dec. 13, 1864,	
Do	Theodore Stauffer	Franklin,	Mar. 8, 1865,	
Company B:				
Captain	Richard C. Horner	Philadelphia	Mar. 8, 1865,	
First Lieutenant	Richard C. Horner	Do	Jan. 13, 1865,	To Captain
Do	John Gayetti	Do	Mar. 8, 1865,	
Do	Christian F. Grumlich	Do	Mar. 8, 1865,	
Second Lieutenant	Christian F. Grumlich	Do	Jan. 13, 1865,	To First Lieutenant
Do	James P. Wolf	Franklin	Mar. 8, 1865,	
Do	D. Emmert Wolf	Do	Mar. 8, 1865,	
Company C:				
Captain	Charles A. Dunkelberg,	Pike	Dec. 20, 1864,	
First Lieutenant	Orlando Keen	Northampton	Dec. 20, 1864,	
Do	Ludwig Herrman	Philadelphia	June 9, 1865,	

ANNUAL REPORT OF THE

ONE HUNDRED AND TWELFTH REGIMENT—Continued.

RANK.	NAME.	CO. OF RESIDENCE.	DATE OF RANK.	REMARKS.
Second Lieutenant.	Jacob Sheets............	Franklin...........	Dec. 20, 1864,	....
Do.............	John Rupert...........	Wayne............	June 9, 1865,	....
Company D:				
Captain............	Joseph W. Winger.....	Franklin...........	Jan. 10, 1865,	....
First Lieutenant.....	Jas. Y. Humphreys....	Philadelphia.....	Jan. 10, 1865,	....
Do..............	William H. Verdier....	Franklin...........	June 1, 1865,	....
Second Lieutenant..	William H. Verdier....	Do	Jan. 11, 1865,	To First Lieutenant......
Do.............	Henry Daniels.........	Do	Mar. 8, 1865,	....
Do.............	Henry Wolf............	Do	June 1, 1865,	....
Company E:				
Captain.............	Bernard Mercer........	Philadelphia.....	Jan. 4, 1865,	....
First Lieutenant.....	Bernard Mercer........	Do	Dec. 20, 1864,	To Captain.............
Do.............	Chas W. Gausline.....	Montgomery.....	Jan. 4, 1865,	....
Do.............	John A. Percy.........	Philadelphia.....	Mar. 8, 1865,	....
Second Lieutenant..	Chas. W. Gausline.....	Montgomery.....	Dec. 20, 1864,	To First Lieutenant......
Do.............	John A. Adams........	Do	Dec. 20, 1864,	....
Do.............	John A. Percy.........	Philadelphia.....	Jan. 4, 1865,	To First Lieutenant.
Do.............	Wm. H. M'Curdy......	Do	Mar. 8, 1865,	....
Do.............	Samuel Hill...........	Do	June 9, 1865,	....
Company F:				
Captain............	George W. Webb.......	Lycoming.........	Mar. 8, 1865,	....
First Lieutenant.....	Stephen H. Witt.......	Chester...........	Nov. 28, 1864,	....
Do..............	John S. Kline..........	Columbia.........	Mar. 8, 1865,	....

EXECUTIVE MILITARY DEPARTMENT. 143

Second Lieutenant	John S. Kline	Columbia	Nov. 28, 1864,	To First Lieutenant	
Do	John Dykeus	Lycoming	Mar. 8, 1865,		
Do	Lloyd T. Brewer	Columbia	June 1, 1865,		
Company G :					
Captain	John Norris	Philadelphia	Nov. 25, 1864,		
First Lieutenant	John M'Gurk	Do	Nov. 25, 1864,		
Second Leutenant	John M'Gurk	Do	Nov. 28, 1864,	To First Lieutenant	
Do	Dennis M. Carroll	Do	Nov. 25, 1864,		
Do	John H. Jenkins	Do	Jan. 11, 1865,		
Company H :					
Captain	George C. Wilson	Huntingdon	Nov. 3, 1864,		
First Lieutenant	Alexander Blackburn	Philadelphia	Mar. 8, 1865,		
Do	Hiram Treher	Franklin	Mar. 8, 1865,	To First Lieutenant	
Second Lieutenant	Alexander Blackburn	Philadelphia	Dec. 20, 1864,		
Do	Mathias Bitner	Franklin	Mar. 8, 1865,		
Company I :					
Captain	William S. Fiss	Philadelphia	Mar. 8, 1865,		
First Lieutenant	William L. Loughlin	Do	Mar. 8, 1865,		
Do	John Guilfoyle	Do	Mar. 8, 1865,		
Second Lieutenant	William H. Lee	Allegheny	Mar. 8, 1865,		
Do	Zaddock M. Morgan	Do	Mar. 8, 1865,		
Company K :					
Captain	John B. Krepps	Fayette	Mar. 8, 1865,		
First Lieutenant	Louis Fisher	Philadelphia	Mar. 8, 1865,		
Do	Peter Heck	Fayette	Mar. 8, 1865,		
Second Lieutenent	Louis Fisher	Philadelphia	Dec. 22, 1864,	To First Lieutenaat	
Do	Charles W. Rush	Fayette	Mar. 8, 1865,		
Do	James S. Darrell	Do	June 1, 1865,		

ONE HUNDRED AND TWELFTH REGIMENT—Continued.

RANK.	NAME.	CO. OF RESIDENCE.	DATE OF RANK.	REMARKS.
Company L:				
Captain............	Joseph L. Iredell.......	Montgomery....	Nov. 30, 1864,	
First Lieutenant....	Martin Litzenberg......	Delaware.........	Nov. 30, 1864,	
Second Lieutenant...	Jeremiah Gilmer.........	Bucks..............	Nov. 30, 1864,	
Do..................	Jerome A. Buck..........	Philadelphia.....	Mar. 8, 1865,	
Do..................	Samuel Long.............	Delaware.........	June 9, 1865,	
Company M:				
Captain............	Albert P. Barber........	Luzerne...........	Mar. 8, 1865,	
First Lieutenant....	Edward H. White........	..Do................	Mar. 8, 1865,	
Second Lieutenant...	James Bucklay..........	Susquehanna ...	Dec. 13, 1864,	
Do..................	Wm. H. Weatherbee....	Luzerne...........	Mar. 8, 1865,	

EXECUTIVE MILITARY DEPARTMENT.

OFFICERS OF THE 112th REGIMENT, TWELFTH CAVALRY.

RANK.	NAME.	CO. OF RESIDENCE	DATE OF RANK.	REMARKS
Colonel	Marcus A. Reno	Dauphin	Dec. 20, 1864,	
Lieutenant Colonel	James A. Congdon	Do	Dec. 20, 1864,	Discharged
Do	Wm. H. M'Allaster	Erie	May 1, 1865,	
Major	Nathaniel Payne	Warren	Jan. 15, 1865,	Mustered out as Captain.
Do	Edson Gerry	Lancaster	Jan. 15, 1865,	
Do	David B. Jenkins	Mifflin	Jan. 15, 1865,	Mustered out as Captain.
Do	Wm. H. M'Allaster	Erie	Mar. 13, 1865,	To Lieutenant Colonel.
Do	John Johnson	Philadelphia	Mar. 13, 1865,	
Do	George W. Henrie	Schuylkill	May 1, 1865,	
Adjutant	James Van Irwin	Juniata	Mar. 2, 1865,	
Commissary	George W. Seibert		Mar. 13, 1865,	
Company A:				
First Lieutenant	Anton Goldsmith	Philadelphia	Jan. 20, 1865,	
Second Lieutenant	Theodore Walton	Do	Jan. 20, 1865,	
Company B:				
Captain	Daniel B. Lewis	Crawford	Jan. 5, 1864,	Hon. disch'd as 2d Lieut. March 21, 1865.
First Lieutenant	H. M. Guild	Do	Jan. 5, 1864,	Resigned February 14, 1865.
Do	John A. Snyder	Do	Feb. 15, 1865,	To First Lieutenant.
Second Lieutenant	John A. Snyder	Do	Jan. 5, 1864,	
Company C:				
Captain	Christian G. Gross	Philadelphia	Mar. 26, 1865,	
Second Lieutenant	James S. Norris	Do	Jan. 20, 1865,	To First Lieutenant Company D.

10 MIL'TARY DEPART.

ANNUAL REPORT OF THE

ONE HUNDRED AND THIRTEENTH REGIMENT—Continued.

RANK.	NAME.	CO. OF RESIDENCE.	DATE OF RANK.	REMARKS.
Company D:				
Captain...............	Augustus Weiss.........	Northampton.....	Mar. 13, 1865,	To Captain.............
First Lieutenant.....	Augustus Weiss.........	Do.............	Jan. 20, 1865,	
Do...................	James S. Norris.........	Philadelphia.....	Mar. 13, 1865,	
Second Lieutenant..	Joseph Ronig...........	Northampton.....	Jan. 20, 1865,	
Company E:				
First Lieutenant.....	Charles P. Kachell.....	Lancaster........	Jan. 20, 1865,	
Second Lieutenant..	Orville C. Wheeler.....		Jan. 20, 1865,	
Company F:				
Captain...............	Thomas Morley.........	Washington......	Jan. 20, 1865,	Discharged April 8, 1865...
First Lieutenant.....	John W. Miller.........		Feb. 13, 1865,	
Second Lieutenant..	Henry E. Gutelius......		Feb. 13, 1865,	
Company G:				
First Lieutenant.....	John H. Black..........	Blair.............	Jan. 20, 1865,	
Second Lieutenant..	Andrew M'Guffy........	Do.............	Jan. 20, 1865,	
Company H:				
First Lieutenant.....	Leon E. Jones...........		Jan. 20, 1865,	
Do...................	Jacob J. Smith..........		Mar. 13, 1865,	
Second Lieutenant..	Jacob J. Smith..........		Jan. 20, 1865,	To First Lieutenant........
Company I:				
Captain...............	John W. Harris.........		Jan. 20, 1865,	
First Lieutenant.....	Charles H. Pearson.....		Nov. 22, 1864,	

Second Lieutenant.	Henry G. Bopp.............	....	Nov. 22, 1864,	....
Company K:				
Captain..................	Addison R. Titus........	Warren............	Jan. 20, 1865,	....
Do	Delos P. Chase	...Do	Mar. 13, 1865,	To Captain.........
First Lieutenant......	Delos P. Chase.........	....Do...............	Jan. 20, 1865,	....
Do	Harvey Russell.........	....Do	Mar. 13, 1865,	To First Lieutenant.
Second Lieutenant..	Harvey Russell........	....Do	Jan. 20, 1865,	....
Do	Stephen B. Sterritt.....	....Do...............	Mar. 13, 1865,	....
Company L:				
Captain.................	O. Budington Tourtelot,	Erie...............	Mar. 13, 1865,	....
First Lieutenant......	O. Budington Tourtelot,	...Do...............	Jan. 20, 1865,	To Captain.........
Do..	Henry A. Drake	...Do...............	Mar. 13, 1865,	....
Second Lieutenant..	Henry A. Drake	...Do	Jan. 20, 1865,	To First Lieutenant.
Do	Bela P. Scovill.........	...Do	Mar. 13, 1865,	....
Company M:				
Captain.................	Henry J. Hite............	Cambria...........	Mar. 13, 1865,	....
First Lieutenant......	Levi Fisher.............	......Do...........	Mar. 13, 1865,	....
Second Lieutenant..	John Herd	......Do......... ..	Mar. 13, 1865,	....

OFFICERS OF THE 114th REGIMENT, INFANTRY.

RANK.	NAME.	CO. OF RESIDENCE.	DATE OF RANK.	REMARKS.
Major............	Henry M. Eddy..........	Philadelphia......	Oct. 31, 1864,	
Company A:				
Captain............	John A. Tricker..........	Philadelphia......	April 15, 1865,	
First Lieutenant....	Robert Gilchrist........	......Do	April 15, 1865,	
Second Lieutenant..	Jacob L. Baugh.........	......Do	June 1, 1865,	
Company B:				
Second Lieutenant..	James B. Simpson.......	Philadelphia......	June 1, 1865,	
Company C:				
Second Lieutenant..	Samuel Smith...........	Philadelphia......	June 1, 1865,	
Company D:				
Captain............	Augustus W. Fix........	Philadelphia......	April 15, 1865,	
First Lieutenant....	William Horrocks........	......Do	April 15, 1865,	
Second Lieutenant..	Harry Hall..............	......Do	June 1, 1865,	
Company E:				
First Lieutenant....	Christian M'Ginley......	Philadelphia......	April 15, 1865,	
Second Lieutenant..	Christian M'Ginley......	......Do	Nov. 21, 1864,	To First Lieutenant.........
Do	Robert C. Kretchman....	......Do	June 1, 1865,	
Company F:				
Second Lieutenant..	John T. Shuster.........	Philadelphia......	June 1, 1865,	

EXECUTIVE MILITARY DEPARTMENT. 149

RANK.	NAME.	CO. OF RESIDENCE.	DATE OF RANK.	REMARKS.
Company G:				
Second Lieutenant..	John Irvin..............	Philadelphia......	June 1, 1865,	....
Company H:				
Captain.............	Benjamin C. Shermer...	Philadelphia......	Sept. 23, 1864,	....
First Lieutenant....	John A. Burk..........	.......Do........	April 15, 1865,	....
Company I:				
First Lieutenant....	Thomas J. Rice........	Philadelphia......	April 15, 1865,	....
Second Lieutenant..	Daniel Hartley........	.......Do........	June 1, 1865,	....
Company K:				
First Lieutenant....	Joshua G. Bates.......	Philadelphia......	Nov. 21, 1864,	....
Second Lieutenant..	Charles Borie.........	.......Do........	June 1, 1865,	....

OFFICERS OF THE 115th REGIMENT, INFANTRY.

RANK.	NAME.	CO. OF RESIDENCE.	DATE OF RANK.	REMARKS.
Company G:				
Captain.............	Jacob B. Meily........	Lebanon..........	Mar. 31, 1864,	....

OFFICERS OF THE 116th REGIMENT, INFANTRY.

RANK.	NAME.	CO. OF RESIDENCE.	DATE OF RANK.	REMARKS.
Colonel	David W. Megraw	Allegheny	June 4, 1865	
Lieutenant Colonel	David W. Megraw	Do	Jan. 18, 1865	To Colonel
Do	Robert J. Alston	Do	June 4, 1865	
Major	David W. Megraw	Do	Jan. 17, 1865	To Lieutenant Colonel
Do	Robert J. Alston	Do	June 3, 1865	To Lieutenant Colonel
Do	Robert J Taggart	Washington	June 4, 1865	
Quartermaster	Zadok B. Springer	Fayette	June 3, 1865	
Company A:				
Captain	George Halpin	Philadelphia	Jan. 23, 1865	
First Lieutenant	Thomas Deitwaler	Do	Jan. 23, 1865	
Company C:				
Captain	William J. Burk	Philadelphia	Feb. 2, 1865	
First Lieutenant	William J. Burk	Do	Oct. 28, 1864	To Captain
Do	Thomas Gray	Do	Feb. 2, 1865	
Company D:				
First Lieutenant	John C. Wright	Philadelphia	Jan. 23, 1865	
Company E:				
Captain	Timothy A. Sloan	Philadelphia	June 22, 1865	To Captain
First Lieutenant	Timothy A. Sloan	Do	May 6, 1865	
Second Lieutenant	Silas Younkin	Somerset	July 1, 1865	
Company F:				
Captain	George Reber	Schuylkill	June 15, 1865	

EXECUTIVE MILITARY DEPARTMENT. 151

First Lieutenant....	George Reber...........	Schuylkill........	July 14, 1865,	To Captain........
Do	Henry S. Kline...........	....Do	June 15, 1865,	
Second Lieutenant..	William M. Wagoner.....	....Do	July 1, 1865,	
Company G :				
Captain........	Saml. G Vanderhyden,	Schuylkill........	June 6, 1865,	
First Lieutenant	William G. Klock........	....Do	June 6, 1865,	
Company H :				
Captain...............	Robert J. Alston........	Allegheny.........	Jan. 17, 1865,	To Major...........
Do	Jacob Forest............	....Do	June 6, 1865,	
First Lieutenant	Jacob Forest............	....Do	Jan. 17, 1865,	To Captain.........
Company I :				
Captain...............	Joseph Warren Yocum,	Montgomery.....	Feb. 18, 1865,	Honorably discharged.....
Do	Robert J. Taggart......	Washington	May 13, 1865,	
Do	Robert P. Brown	Allegheny.........	June 4, 1865,	
First Lieutenant....	Robert J. Taggart	Washington......	Feb. 18, 1865,	To Captain.........
Do	Robert P. Brown........	Allegheny.........	May 13, 1865,	To Captain.........
Company K :				
Captain...............	James D. Cope	Fayette.............	June 22, 1865,	

OFFICERS OF THE 117th REGIMENT, THIRTEENTH CAVALRY.

RANK.	NAME.	CO. OF RESIDENCE.	DATE OF RANK.	REMARKS.
Quartermaster......	Anthony Wise..........	Bucks.............	Dec. 28, 1864,	
Commissary	Daniel A. Callahan....	Philadelphia......	Feb. 11, 1865,	
Company A :				
Captain...............	David M'Neil...........	Philadelphia......	Jan. 4, 1865,	
First Lieutenant	John Lawton	Delaware..........	Jan. 4, 1865,	
Company B :				
Captain...............	Curtis H. Eldridge......	Lycoming.........	April 20, 1865,	
First Lieutenant	George M'Lain..........	Philadelphia......	April 20, 1865,	
Second Lieutenant..	Henry Brunner........	York...............	April 20, 1865,	
Company D ;				
Captain...............	J. M. Bell..............	Huntingdon	Feb. 8, 1865,	
First Lieutenant	Frank Y. M'Donald.....		April 6, 1864,	Discharged December 3, 1864.....
Do	Henry N. Baker........		Nov 15, 1864,	
Second Lieutenant..	George W. Cruse.......	Blair	Nov. 15, 1864,	
Company E :				
Captain...............	George R. Maguire.....	Philadelphia......	Feb. 7, 1865,	
First Lieutenant	Daniel Caldwell.........	Montgomery.....	Jan. 12, 1865,	
Second Lieutenant..	James D. Patterson	Bucks.............	Feb. 13, 1865,	
Company G :				
Captain...............	Robert Brown	Lycoming........	Nov. 26, 1864,	
First Lieutenant	John R. Smith..........	....Do	Nov. 26, 1864,	
Second Lieutenant..	James M. Antes........	....Do	Nov. 26, 1864,	

EXECUTIVE MILITARY DEPARTMENT. 153

Company H:				
Captain............	Albert H. Glassmire....	Schuylkill.........	Feb. 13, 1865,	....
First Lieutenant ...	E. F. Smith............	....Do	Feb. 13, 1865,	....
Second Lieutenant..	John Cunius............	Luzerne............	Feb. 13, 1865,	....
Company K:				
Captain............	John W. Berks	Philadelphia......	Nov. 15, 1864,	....
First Lieutenant	Sam'l W. Sollenberger,	Cumberland......	Nov. 15, 1864,	....
Second Lieutenant..	William M. Corson......	Montgomery.....	Nov. 15, 1864,	....
Company L:				
Captain............	Edward O'Shea.........	Philadelphia. ...	July 8, 1863,	....
First Lieutenant ...	William O'Connor......	..... Do	July 8, 1863,	....
Company M:				
Captain............	Thomas Marks.........	Philadelphia......	Nov. 27, 1864,	....
First Lieutenant ...	Thomas Marks.........	..... Do	Nov. 15, 1864,	To Captain......
Do	John Leahey...........	Montgomery.....	Nov. 29, 1864,	....
Second Lieutenant.	John A. Turner.........	Philadelphia......	Feb. 13, 1865,	....

OFFICERS OF THE 118th REGIMENT, INFANTRY.

RANK.	NAME.	CO. OF RESIDENCE.	DATE OF RANK.	REMARKS.
Company A:				
Captain............	George W. Moore.......	Philadelphia.....	Mar. 28, 1865,	....
First Lieutenant....	Wm. T. Godwin......	......Do........	Nov. 7, 1864,	....
Company B:				
First Lieutenant....	Thomas Kelly.........	Philadelphia.....	Mar. 28, 1865,	....
Company C:				
First Lieutenant....	James Donnelly........	Philadelphia.....	Mar. 28, 1865,	....
Company E:				
Captain............	Henry Conner.........	Philadelphia.....	Mar. 28, 1865,	....
First Lieutenant....	Robert Paschall.......	......Do........	Nov. 7, 1864,	....
Company F:				
Captain............	John Scott............	Philadelphia.....	Oct. 30, 1864,	....
Do	John L. Bell.........	......Do........	Mar. 28, 1865,	....
Company G:				
Captain............	John R. White........	Philadelphia.....	Jan. 6, 1865,	....
First Lieutenant....	Jonas Brubaker..	......Do........	Jan. 6, 1865,	....
Company H:				
First Lieutenant....	Henry Conner.........	Philadelphia.....	Nov. 7, 1864,	....
Company K:				
Captain.	Isaac H. Seesholtz	Philadelphia.....	Oct. 30, 1864,	....

EXECUTIVE MILITARY DEPARTMENT. 155

OFFICERS OF THE 119th REGIMENT, INFANTRY.

RANK.	NAME.	CO. OF RESIDENCE.	DATE OF RANK.	REMARKS.
Colonel	Gideon Clarke	Philadelphia	Jan. 13, 1864,	
Lieutenant Colonel	William C. Gray	Delaware	May 13, 1864,	
Major	Edwin A. Landell	Philadelphia	June 9, 1865,	
Adjutant	D. S. Hassinger	Do	April 3, 1865,	
Company C:				
Captain	George R. Dickson	Philadelphia	April 21, 1865,	
First Lieutenant	George R. Dickson	Do	May 11, 1864,	To Captain.
Do	Robert M'Kee	Do	April 21, 1865,	
Company D:				
Second Lieutenant	Rudolph Woerner	Philadelphia	June 9, 1865,	
Company E:				
Second Lieutenant	Jacob Bardsley	Philadelphia	June 9, 1865,	
Company F:				
First Lieutenant	Rowan Foulke	Philadelphia	April 3, 1865,	
Company G:				
Second Lieutenant	John J. Williams	Philadelphia	June 9, 1865,	
Company H:				
Second Lieutenant	Samuel Schlotterer	Philadelphia	June 9, 1865,	
Company I:				
Captain	George Conrow	Philadelphia	June 9, 1865,	
First Lieutenant	George Conrow	Do	Jan. 21, 1865,	To Captain.
Do	Henry Shelley	Do	June 9, 1865,	
Company K:				
Second Lieutenant	George W. Johnson	Philadelphia	June 9, 1865,	

OFFICERS OF THE 121st REGIMENT, INFANTRY.

RANK.	NAME.	CO. OF RESIDENCE.	DATE OF RANK.	REMARKS.
Major..................	West Funk...............	Philadelphia......	Sept. 7, 1864,	....
Company B:				
Captain............	Joseph Rylands.........	Philadelphia......	Jan. 6, 1865,	....
Company C:				
Captain............	Joshua L. Childs........	Philadelphia......	Dec. 22, 1864,	....
First Lieutenant.....	James Culbertson........	......Do	Dec. 22, 1864,	....
Company E:				
Captain............	William W. Strong......	Philadelphia......	Jan. 1, 1865,	....
First Lieutenant.....	Richard A. Dempsey.....	......Do	Jan. 1, 1865,	....
Company F:				
Captain............	Daniel B. Levier........	Philadelphia......	Jan. 21, 1865,	....
First Lieutenant.....	James Davidson.........	......Do	Jan. 21, 1865,	....
Company G:				
Captain............	James H. Watson........	Philadelphia......	Dec. 7, 1864,	....
First Lieutenant.....	Joseph A. Bastion........	......Do	Dec. 7, 1864,	....
Do	John M'Connell...........	......Do	May 25, 1865,	....
Company H:				
Captain............	Richard H Shute........	Philadelphia......	Feb. 1, 1865,	....
First Lieutenant.....	Joseph R. Davis..........	......Do	Feb. 1, 1865,	....
Second Lieutenant..	Charles M. Wills.........	......Do	Feb. 1, 1865,	....

OFFICERS OF THE 138th REGIMENT, INFANTRY.

RANK.	NAME.	CO. OF RESIDENCE.	DATE OF RANK.	REMARKS.
Lieutenant Colonel..	Lewis A. May........	Bedford........	Jan. 17, 1865,	....
Major................	Simon Deckerhoff....	....Do	June 28, 1865,	....
Chaplain............	John W. Feight......	....Do	Jan. 12, 1865,	....
Company A:				
Second Lieutenant..	Daniel A. Reiff.......	Montgomery.....	Mar. 25, 1865,	....
Company B:				
Second Lieutenant..	David M. M'Knight ...	Montgomery.....	Oct. 1, 1864,	....
Company D:				
Captain..............	Oliver Horton	Bedford........	Feb. 4, 1865,	....
First Lieutenant.....	Emanuel Fisher......	....Do	Feb. 4, 1865,	....
Company E:				
Captain..............	Reuben W. Cooke.....	Bedford........	June 28, 1865,	....
Company F:				
Captain..............	Martin S. Boitz	Bedford........	Feb. 9, 1865,	....
First Lieutenant.....	Christopher P. Calhoun,	....Do	Feb. 9, 1865,	....
Second Lieutenant...	Levi Cook............	....Do	May 5, 1865,	....
Company G:				
Captain..............	George W. Mullen....	Adams..........	Mar. 23, 1865,	....
First Lieutenant	George W. Mullen....	....Do	Dec. 29, 1864,	....

ONE HUNDRED AND THIRTY-EIGHTH REGIMENT—Continued.

RANK.	NAME.	CO. OF RESIDENCE.	DATE OF RANK.	REMARKS.
Company I:				
Captain	William C. Ensley	Montgomery	April 6, 1865,	
First Lieutenant	Osceola Lewis	Do	April 6, 1865,	
Second Lieutenant	George H. Rees	Do	April 6, 1865,	
Company K:				
Captain	Jonathan P. Iredell	Montgomery	May 18, 1865,	

OFFICERS OF THE 139th REGIMENT, INFANTRY.

RANK.	NAME.	CO. OF RESIDENCE.	DATE OF RANK.	REMARKS.
Major............	James M'Gregor.........	Allegheny.........	Dec. 20, 1864,	....
Company A:				
First Lieutenant....	Joseph T. Black.........	Mercer......	Jan. 14, 1865,	....
Do	James S. Maguire.......	......Do	Mar. 26, 1865,	....
Second Lieutenant..	James S. Maguire.......	......Do	Jan. 15, 1865,	To First Lieutenant.........
Company B:				
Captain.............	George A. Williams.....	Armstrong.........	Nov. 28, 1864,	Hon. discharged, to date May 15, 1865...
First Lieutenant....	Andrew J. Stitt	......Do	Nov. 28, 1864,	....
Company C:				
First Lieutenant....	Alexander J. Hamilton,	....	Mar. 1, 1865,	....
Company D:				
Captain.............	Michael Mullin............	Allegheny.........	Mar. 1, 1865,	....
Do	Joseph T. Black.........	Mercer.........	Mar. 26, 1865,	Killed March 25, 1865.........
Company G:				
First Lieutenant....	Frank Goodin.............	Allegheny.........	Aug. 25, 1865,	....
Company I:				
Captain.............	John C. Sample.........	Allegheny.........	Jan. 5, 1865,	Hon. discharged, to date May 15, 1865...
First Lieutenant....	Charles J. Swanley.....	......Do	Jan. 5, 1865,	....
Company K:				
Captain.............	William L. Pettit.......	Allegheny.........	Dec. 20, 1864,	....
First Lieutenant....	John A. Heiber.........	......Do	Dec. 20, 1864,	....

OFFICERS OF THE 140th REGIMENT, INFANTRY.

RANK.	NAME.	CO. OF RESIDENCE.	DATE OF RANK.	REMARKS.
Adjutant............	John S. Bryan............	Beaver......	Dec. 6, 1864,	
Quartermaster......	Robert B. Parkinson....	Allegheny......	Dec. 6, 1864,	
Company A:				
Captain............	John A. Burns...........	Greene............	Dec. 18, 1864,	
First Lieutenant....	Mark G. Spragg.........	....Do	Dec. 18, 1864,	
Second Lieutenant..	Charles T. Hedge........	....Do	Dec. 18, 1864,	
Company B:				
Captain............	R. C. Craig	Mercer............	Dec. 18, 1864,	
First Lieutenant....	John Satterfield........	....Do	Dec. 18, 1864,	
Second Lieutenant..	John Fox	....Do	Dec. 18, 1864,	
Company C:				
Captain.....	John M. Ray............	Washington	Dec. 4, 1864,	
First Lieutenant....	Wm. J. Cunningham ...	Westmoreland ...	Dec. 4, 1864,	
Second Lieutenant..	John W. Wiley..........	Washington	Dec. 18, 1864,	
Company E:				
Captain............	Jesse T. Power.	Washington	Dec. 14, 1864,	
First Lieutenant....	William D. Lank........	....Do	Dec. 14, 1864,	
Company G:				
Captain............	Wilson N. Paxton.......	Washington	April 16, 1865,	Mustered out of service, May 15, 1865...
Do	John R. Paxton.........	....Do..... ...	May 16, 1865,	
First Lieutenant....	John R. Paxton.........	....Do	April 16, 1865,	To Captain.......
Company I:				
Second Lieutenant..	William A. McMillan...	Beaver......	Dec. 18, 1864,	

OFFICERS OF THE 141st REGIMENT, INFANTRY.

RANK.	NAME.	CO. OF RESIDENCE.	DATE OF RANK.	REMARKS.
Lieutenant Colonel.	Joseph H Horton......	Bradford........	Feb. 28, 1865,	....
Major...............	Joseph H. Horton.....	Do	Jan. 31, 1865,	To Lieutenant Colonel......
Do...............	Charles Mercur........	......Do	Feb. 28, 1865,	....
Quartermaster.......	Charles Cash.........	......Do	Oct. 25, 1864,	....
Company A:				
Captain.............	Joseph H. Hurst.......	Bradford........	Feb. 28, 1865,	....
First Lieutenant....	James W. Alderson....	......Do	Feb. 28, 1865,	....
Company C:				
First Lieutenant....	Martin V. Codding....	....	April 19, 1865,	....
Company D:				
Captain.............	Marcus E. Warner.....	Bradford........	Aug. 7, 1864,	....
First Lieutenant....	H. J. Hudson..........	....	Jan. 31, 1865,	....
Company E:				
Captain.............	Mason Long...........	Bradford........	June 28, 1864,	....
First Lieutenant....	John M. Jackson......	......Do	Jan. 2, 1865,	....
Company F:				
Captain.............	Nelson J. Hawley.....	Susquehanna ...	Oct. 5, 1864,	....
Company G:				
Captain.............	William T. Lobb......	....	Jan. 8, 1865,	....
First Lieutenant....	John T. R. Seagraves..	....	Jan. 8, 1865,	....
Company I:				
Captain.............	John G. Brown	Bradford........	Dec. 20, 1864,	....
First Lieutenant....	John S. Frink.........	......Do	Dec. 20, 1864,	....

11 MILITARY DEPART.

OFFICERS OF THE 142d REGIMENT, INFANTRY.

RANK.	NAME.	CO. OF RESIDENCE.	DATE OF RANK.	REMARKS.
Colonel	Horatio N. Warren	Mercer	June 3, 1865,	
Major	Harry G. Elder	Somerset	May 16, 1865,	
Adjutant	H. Warren Stinson		Dec. 11, 1864,	
Company A:				
Captain	Martin A. Gibson	Mercer	June 3, 1865,	
First Lieutenant	C. B. Thompson	Do	June 3, 1865,	
Second Lieutenant	A. H. Goble	Do	June 3, 1865,	
Company B:				
Second Lieutenant	Urbanus Hubbs	Westmoreland	June 3, 1865,	
Company C:				
Captain	Jacob R. Walter	Somerset	June 3, 1865,	
First Lieutenant	Charles F. Hunter	Do	June 3, 1865,	
Second Lieutenant	D. Young	Do	June 3, 1865,	
Company D:				
Second Lieutenant	Oliver Shaver	Somerset	June 3, 1865,	
Company F:				
Captain	Joseph Lepley	Somerset	June 3, 1865,	
First Lieutenant	Jacob Jorn	Do	June 3, 1865,	
Second Lieutenant	Samuel Hoon	Do	June 3, 1865,	
Company G:				
Second Lieutenant	Joseph Heckman	Monroe	June 3, 1865,	

Company I: Second Lieutenant..	Oliver P. Young........	Venango.........	June 3, 1865,
Company K: Second Lieutenant..	Samuel Decker..........	Luzerne.........	June 3, 1865,

OFFICERS OF THE 143d REGIMENT, INFANTRY.

RANK.	NAME.	CO. OF RESIDENCE.	DATE OF RANK.	REMARKS.
Lieutenant Colonel.	George N. Reichard....	Luzerne........	June 1, 1865,	....
Adjutant................	Charles H. Campbell...	......Do.......	Sept. 8, 1864,	....
Quartermaster.......	William D. Warfel......	......Do.......	May 17, 1865,	....
Company A:				
Second Lieutenant..	Wm. H. Bennett.........	Luzerne........	June 1, 1865,	....
Company D:				
Captain................	Milton T. Bailey........	Luzerne........	April 26, 1865,	....
First Lieutenant	Wilbur F. Rice...........	......Do.......	April 26, 1865,	....
Second Lieutenant..	Patrick De Lacey.......	...... Do.......	April 26, 1865,	....
Company E:				
First Lieutenant....	Herbert N. Greenslitt..	Luzerne........	Jan. 1, 1865,	....
Second Lieutenant..	Levi B. Tompkins.......	......Do.......	Jan. 1, 1865,	....
Company F:				
Second Lieutenant..	Nathaniel J. M. Heck..	Luzerne........	Sept. 8, 1864,	....
Company G:				
First Lieutenant....	Patrick Murphy.........	Luzerne	Sept. 15, 1864,	....
Company I:				
Captain	Jarius Kauff.............	Luzerne........	Oct. 15, 1864,	....
Do	Harlan Potter............	......Do.......	Mar. 14, 1865,	....
First Lieutenant	Harlan Potter............	......Do.......	Nov. 23, 1864,	To Captain.
Do	Wm H. Blain...........	......Do.......	Mar. 14, 1865,	....

Do..................	Simon Hubler..........	......Do......	......	June 1, 1865,
Company K:				
First Lieutenant.....	Benjamin Walters.......	Mifflin.......	Dec. 18, 1864,	
Second Lieutenant...	Horace C. Harding......	Wyoming.......	Jan. 10, 1865,	

OFFICERS OF THE 145th REGIMENT, INFANTRY.

RANK.	NAME.	CO. OF RESIDENCE.	DATE OF RANK.	REMARKS.
Colonel	David B. M'Creary	Erie	Jan. 17, 1865	
Lieutenant Colonel	Charles M. Lynch	Do	Jan. 17, 1865	
Major	James H. Hamlin	Do	Jan. 17, 1865	
Quartermaster	Jonathan Spaulding	Do	May 22, 1865	
Company A:				
First Lieutenant	Charles S. Steadman	Erie	May 22, 1865	
Company B:				
Captain	Martin O. Way	Erie	April 26, 1865	
First Lieutenant	Samuel M. Birchfield	Do	April 26, 1864	
Second Lieutenant	Albert Dunn	Do	April 26, 1865	
Company C:				
Second Lieutenant	John M. Fargo		Sept. 23, 1864	
Company E:				
First Lieutenant	Delos Clemmons		Dec. 19, 1864	
Company F:				
Captain	Lewis B. Carlile	Warren	June 18, 1864	Honorably disch'd, to date May 15, 1865.
Do	Charles C. Merritt	Do	May 22, 1865	
First Lieutenant	John L. Cohell	Do	May 22, 1865	
Company G:				
Second Lieutenant	Stephen A. Osborne		Oct. 21, 1864	

EXECUTIVE MILITARY DEPARTMENT. 167

Company H:				
First Lieutenant	William S. Trimble	....	....	Oct. 5, 1864,
Second Lieutenant	Nathan P. Kinsley	....	....	Oct. 5, 1864,
Company I:				
Captain	George A. Evans	....	Erie	Jan. 17, 1865,

OFFICERS OF THE 147th REGIMENT, INFANTRY.

RANK.	NAME.	CO. OF RESIDENCE.	DATE OF RANK.	REMARKS.
Colonel...............	John Craig............	Carbon	June 14, 1865,	
Major..................	Wm. J. Mackey........	Philadelphia......	June 14, 1865,	
Company A :				
Captain..............	George F. Dible........	Allegheny.........	Nov. 1, 1864,	
First Lieutenant...	Samuel Eccles	....Do............	April 7, 1865,	
Second Lieutenant.	John H. Cunliffe.....	Philadelphia......	July 8, 1865,	
Company B :				
Captain...............	Alfred H. W. Creigh....	Huntingdon	Oct. 26, 1864,	
First Lieutenant	Robert B. Thompson....	......Do..........	Oct. 26, 1864,	
Second Lieutenant.	David Heffner.........	......Do.........	July 8, 1865,	
Company C :				
Captain...............	Alexander Youngst.....	Luzerne...........	June 14, 1865,	
First Lieutenant	David Bryan............	....Do............	April 9, 1865,	
Second Lieutenant.	John Grubb.............	Chester...........	July 8, 1865,	
Company D :				
Second Lieutenant.	Edward Riley..........	Luzerne...........	July 8, 1865,	
Company E :				
Captain...............	William M. Clark......	Chester...........	Feb. 3, 1865,	
First Lieutenant	William M. Clark......	....Do............	Nov. 1, 1864,	To Captain.......
Do	Edward Welsh.........	....Do............	Feb. 3, 1865,	
Second Lieutenant.	Robert J. Potter........	Westmoreland ...	July 8, 1865,	

EXECUTIVE MILITARY DEPARTMENT.

Company F:				
First Lieutenant....	John F. Pettit............	Luzerne.........	Jan. 14, 1865,	....
Second Lieutenant.	John Duser.............	....Do	July 8, 1865,	....
Company G:				
Second Lieutenant.	Franklin M. Stork......	Snyder.........	July 8, 1865,	....
Company H:				
Second Lieutenant.	Edward J. Schwoly.....	Luzerne.........	July 8, 1865,	....
Company I:				
Captain..............	Thomas Fair............	Philadelphia.....	Oct. 7, 1864,	....
First Lieutenant...	Isaac D. Whitmer.......	Snyder.........	Oct. 7, 1864,	....
Do	George Henry	Philadelphia.....	Feb. 3, 1865,	....
Second Lieutenant,	Wm. T. Richardson....	.....Do	July 8, 1865,	....

OFFICERS OF THE 148th REGIMENT, INFANTRY.

RANK.	NAME.	CO. OF RESIDENCE.	DATE OF RANK.	REMARKS.
Colonel............	James F. Weaver.......	Centre.......	June 1, 1865,	....
Lieutenant Colonel.	James F. Weaver.......	..Do.......	May 6, 1865,	To Colonel.......
Do	George A. Bayard.......	..Do.......	June 1, 1865,	....
Major.............	James F. Weaver.......	..Do.......	Feb. 1, 1865,	To Lieutenant Colonel.....
Do	George A. Bayard......	..Do.......	May 6, 1865,	To Lieutenant Colonel.....
Do	Silas J. Marlin.........	Jefferson......	June 1, 1865,	....
Adjutant..........	Charles A. Ramsey.....	Mifflin	April 15, 1865,	....
Company B:				
Captain...........	William D. Harper.....	Centre	Feb. 1, 1865,	....
First Lieutenant...	James E. M'Cartney..	..Do	Feb. 1, 1865,	....
Do	David H. Swyers......	..Do	Mar. 1, 1865,	....
Second Lieutenant..	Thomas T. Taylor......	..Do	June 1, 1865,	....
Company C:				
Captain...........	Samuel Everhart......	Centre.......	Mar. 1, 1865,	Killed........
Do	John F. Benner.......	..Do........	April 15, 1865,	To Captain.......
First Lieutenant...	John F. Benner.......	..Do.......	Mar. 1, 1865,	....
Do	Daniel Shuey.........	..Do.......	April 15, 1865,	....
Second Lieutenant..	William H. Mayer.....	..Do.......	June 1, 1865,	....
Company F:				
Captain...........	Jacob Breon..........	Centre.......	Feb. 1, 1865,	....
First Lieutenant...	J. Asher Sankey......	..Do.......	Dec. 1, 1864,	....
Do	William Luear........	..Do.......	April 15, 1865,	....
Second Lieutenant..	William Mackey.......	..Do.......	May 18, 1865,	....

EXECUTIVE MILITARY DEPARTMENT. 171

Company G:				
Captain	Isaac Lytle	Centre	Dec. 12, 1864,	Resigned on account of wounds
Do	John H. Harpster	.Do	Jan. 25, 1865,	
First Lieutenant	John H. Harpster	....Do	Dec. 12, 1864,	To Captain
Do	Joseph Fox	....Do	Jan. 25, 1865,	
Second Lieutenant	Joseph Fox	....Do	Dec. 12, 1864,	To First Lieutenant
Do	John W. Stuart	....Do	Jan. 25, 1865,	
Company H:				
Captain	Henry H. Montgomery	Centre	May 6, 1865,	
First Lieutenant	Alexander Gibb	....Do	May 6, 1865,	
Second Lieutenant	J. A. J. Fugate	....Do	June 1, 1865,	
Company I:				
Captain	Junius F. Crain	Jefferson	June 1, 1865,	
First Lieutenant	Frank W. Clark	....Do	June 1, 1865,	
Second Lieutenant	Thompson Douglass	....Do	June 1, 1865,	

OFFICERS OF THE 149th REGIMENT, INFANTRY.

RANK.	NAME.	CO. OF RESIDENCE.	DATE OF RANK.	REMARKS.
Colonel	John Irvin	Clearfield	Jan. 28, 1865,	
Lieutenant Colonel	James Glenn	Allegheny	Jan. 28, 1865,	
Major	Edward S. Osborne	Luzerne	Jan. 28, 1865,	
Company A :				
Captain	Benjamin H. Warriner		Nov. 14, 1864,	
First Lieutenant	John Walbridge		Nov. 14, 1864,	
Second Lieutenant	George D. Brook		Mar. 9, 1865,	
Company B :				
Captain	John L. Rex	Clearfield	Dec. 22, 1864,	
First Lieutenant	Albert B. Cole	Do	Dec. 22, 1864,	
Do	Milton M'Clure	Do	Feb. 7, 1865,	Killed in action February 6, 1865.
Second Lieutenant	Newton Reed	Do	May 15, 1865,	
Company C :				
Second Lieutenant	Henry Hoffman	Lebanon	April 1, 1865,	
Company D :				
Captain	William M. Dalgleish	Allegheny	June 14, 1865,	
First Lieutenant	John A. Snodgrass	Do	June 14, 1865,	
Second Lieutenant	Frank C. Dorrington	Do	June 14, 1865,	
Company F :				
Captain	Myron Fellows	Luzerne	Jan. 28, 1865,	Discharged ....[May 15, 1865.
Do	James Post	Do	April 1, 1865,	Hon. disch'd as First Lieutenant to date
First Lieutenant	James Post	Do	Jan. 28, 1865,	To Captain.

EXECUTIVE MILITARY DEPARTMENT.

Do................	William Buckalew.......	Luzerne........	April 1, 1865,	
Second Lieutenant.	William Buckalew.......	Do	Jan. 28, 1865,	To First Lieutenant.......
Do................	Lewis M. Crevling.......	Do.............	May 15, 1865,	
Company G:				
Captain............	Alonzo B. Horton........	Potter.........	April 1, 1865,	
First Lieutenant...	John T. Miller............	Do.............	April 1, 1865,	
Second Lieutenant.	Henry Fissel	Perry..........	May 15, 1865,	
Company K:				
Captain............	Charles F. Barclay......	Cameron.......	May 16, 1865,	
First Lieutenant....	A. l. Harvey.............	Potter.........	May 16, 1865,	
Second Lieutenant.	John V. Brown..........	Do.............	May 16, 1865,	

OFFICERS OF THE 150th REGIMENT, INFANTRY.

RANK.	NAME.	CO. OF RESIDENCE.	DATE OF RANK.	REMARKS.
Colonel............	George W. Jones.........	Philadelphia......	June 15, 1865,	
Lieutenant Colonel..	George W. Jones.........	....Do......	May 16, 1865,	To Colonel......
Do	John W. Sigler............	Crawford.........	June 15, 1865,	
Major............	Benjamin F. Topham...	Philadelphia......	June 15, 1865,	
Chaplain..........	C. Comfort.	M'Kean.........	Nov. 28, 1864,	
Company A:				
Second Lieutenant..	Henry Folwell...........	Philadelphia......	June 15, 1865,	
Company B:				
Captain........	Alfred J. Rorer.........	Philadelphia......	June 15, 1865,	
First Lieutenant	Edward L. Dickerson...	......Do	June 15, 1865,	
Second Lieutenant...	Joseph Maxwell.........	......Do	June 15, 1865,	
Company D:				
Captain............	Sam'l H. Himmelright...	Union............	Oct. 21, 1864,	
First Lieutenant	John A. Hanck.........	.Do............	Oct. 21, 1864,	
Second Lieutenant...	James Cummings	...Do............	June 15, 1865,	
Company E:				
Captain............	Henry Lukens...........	Philadelphia......	June 15, 1865,	
First Lieutenant....	Franklin Taggard	...Do	June 15, 1865,	
Second Lieutenant...	John A. Smyth	Lancaster.........	June 15, 1865,	
Company F:				
Captain	Charles F. Street.........	Philadelphia......	June 15, 1865,	
First Lieutenant....	John D. Harris...........	...Do	June 15, 1865,	
Second Lieutenant...	Levi Munshower........	Chester.........	June 15, 1865,	

EXECUTIVE MILITARY DEPARTMENT. 175

Company G:				
Second Lieutenant.	Daniel Beekwith........	M'Kean.........	June 15, 1865,	
Company H:				
Captain............	Charles L. Reisinger....	Crawford.........	Dec. 16, 1864,	Mustered out of service for physical disa-
Do	Benj. W. Topping.......	......Do	June 1, 1865,	[bility.
First Lieutenant....	Benj. W. Topping.......	...... Do	Dec. 16 1864,	To Captain............
Do	James T. Reed...........	......Do	June 1, 1865,	
Second Lieutenant..	Lafayette Derby.........	......Do	June 15, 1865,	
Company I:				
Captain...........	Gilbert Gordon...........	Crawford.........	June 15, 1865,	
First Lieutenant....	Francis A. Magee........	......Do	June 15, 1865,	
Second Lieutenant..	Francis Gilson..........	......Do	June 15, 1865,	
Company K:				
First Lieutenant....	Thomas L. M'Vey.......	Venango.........	Mar. 11, 1865,	
Second Lieutenant..	William Hontz...........	......Do	Mar. 11, 1865,	

OFFICERS OF THE 153d REGIMENT, THIRD ARTILLERY.

RANK.	NAME.	CO. OF RESIDENCE.	DATE OF RANK.	REMARKS.
Major.............	John A. Blake............	Lancaster........	Sept. 1, 1865,	....
Company B:				
Second Lieutenant..	Uriah Johnston..........	Philadelphia......	April 12, 1865,	....
Company C:				
Captain...............	Robert W. Bickley......	Philadelphia.....	May 23, 1865,	....
First Lieutenant....	Daniel W. Shelley......	Cumberland......	May 23, 1865,	....
Do...............	Franklin Martin.........	Do............	June 13, 1865,	....
Second Lieutenant..	Amos E. Fetrow..........	Do............	May 23, 1865,	....
Do...............	Philip S. Skettel.........	Do............	July 30, 1865,	....
Company D:				
First Lieutenant....	Sylvester W. Marshall..	Northumberland,	July 5, 1865,	....
Second Lieutenant..	Loren M. Leonard.......	Bradford..........	Aug. 7, 1865,	....
Company E:				
Captain...............	Erskine H. Miles.........	Huntingdon......	Feb. 13, 1865,	....
Do...............	George S. Roberts........	Philadelphia.....	Sept. 9, 1865,	....
First Lieutenant....	George S. Roberts........	Do............	Feb. 13, 1865,	To Captain.........
Do...............	Hiram T. Taylor..........	Lycoming.........	Sept. 9, 1865,	....
Second Lieutenant..	William G. Burwell.....	Schuylkill........	Feb. 13, 1865,	....
Do...............	Hiram T. Taylor..........	Lycoming.........	Feb. 13, 1865,	To First Lieutenant..
Company F:				
Captain...............	Joseph N. Porter.........	Schuylkill........	Sept. 1, 1865,	....
First Lieutenant....	John W. Blake............	Huntingdon......	Sept. 1, 1865,	....

EXECUTIVE MILITARY DEPARTMENT. 177

First Lieutenant....	James O. Allen.........	Philadelphia.....	Jan. 9, 1865,	
Do	William Winckle........	....Do	Sept. 1, 1865,	To First Lieutenant......
Second Lieutenant..	William Winckle........	....Do	Feb. 21, 1865,	
Do	J. B. Shoup.............	....Do	Jan. 9, 1865,	
Do	William C. M'Cormick,	Lehigh..........	Sept. 1, 1865,	
Company H:				
Second Lieutenant.	Byron Pope	Philadelphia.....	June 2, 1865,	
Company I:				
First Lieutenant....	James B. Carpenter....	Philadelphia.....	Sept. 1, 1865,	
Second Lieutenant..	Joseph B. Walters......	Bucks...........	Sept. 1, 1865,	
Company K:				
Second Lieutenant.	George H. Harper......	Philadelphia.....	April 29, 1865,	
Do	Henry Wilkinson........	Philadelphia.....	June 29, 1965,	
Company L:				
Second Lieutenant.	Henry A. Adams	Philadelphia.....	May 29, 1865,	
Company M:				
Second Lieutenant.	Robert Barr.............	Philadelphia.....	April 1, 1865,	
Do	John W. Kaye...........	....Do	April 30, 1865,	

12 MILITARY DEPART.

OFFICERS OF THE 155th REGIMENT, INFANTRY.

RANK.	NAME.	CO. OF RESIDENCE.	DATE OF RANK.	REMARKS.
Major............	John Andrew Cline......	Armstrong.......	Aug. 31, 1863,	....
Company A:				
Captain...........	Edwin A. Montooth....	Allegheny........	May 15, 1865,	....
Company C:				
First Lieutenant....	John H. Irwin...........	Allegheny........	Jan. 1, 1865,	....
Second Lieutenant..	Thomas B. Dunn.........	Do	Jan. 1, 1865,	....
Do................	Joseph M. Cargo.........	Do	April 2, 1865,	....
Company D:				
Captain.............	Alexander Carson.......	Allegheny........	Mar. 10, 1865,	....
Do	John C. Sweeney.........	Do	Mar. 11, 1865,	....
Second Lieutenant..	William Shore...........	Do	Mar. 11, 1865,	....
Company F:				
Second Lieutenant..	John Ralston.............	Allegheny........	May 10, 1865,	....
Company I:				
Captain.............	John T. Bell..............	Jefferson.........	July 2, 1864,	....
First Lieutenant....	James D. Pierce..........	Allegheny........	Mar. 30, 1865,	....
Second Lieutenant..	Thomas C. Anderson....	Do	Mar. 30, 1865,	....
Company K:				
Captain.............	Benjamin Huey...........	Allegheny........	Jan. 1, 1865,	....
First Lieutenant....	J. A. H. Foster...........	Do	Jan. 1, 1865,	....
Second Lieutenant..	David Porter Marshall.	Armstrong	Feb. 16, 1865,	....

OFFICERS OF THE 157th REGIMENT, INFANTRY.

RANK.	NAME.	CO. OF RESIDENCE.	DATE OF RANK.	REMARKS.
Lieutenant Colonel..	Edmund T. Tiers.........	Philadelphia......	Dec. 1, 1864,	
Major.................	Thomas E. Carter........	......Do...............	Dec. 1, 1864,	
Company A:				
Captain...............	Alexander Gray..........	Philadelphia......	Sept. 24, 1864,	
First Lieutenant.....	George R. Eckendorff....	......Do...............	Sept. 24, 1864,	
Do................	Edward J. Collins........	......Do...............	April 28, 1865,	
Company B:				
Captain...............	William F. Crane........	Philadelphia......	Dec. 1, 1864,	Honorably discharged May 8, 1865........
First Lieutenant.....	William Grist............	......Do...............	Dec. 1, 1864,	Hon. disch'd, to take effect May 15, 1865.
Company C:				
Captain...............	Charles H. Addicks.....	Philadelphia......	Dec. 1, 1864,	
First Lieutenant.....	Thomas S. Marsh........	......Do...............	Feb. 1, 1865,	
Do................	John W. Frambes........	......Do...............	April 28, 1865,	

OFFICERS OF THE 159th REGIMENT, FOURTEENTH CAVALRY.

RANK.	NAME.	CO. OF RESIDENCE.	DATE OF RANK.	REMARKS.
Lieutenant Colonel.	John M. Daily	Armstrong	June 7, 1865,	
Major	William W. Miles	Erie	Nov. 12, 1864,	
Do	John Bird	Allegheny	June 7, 1865,	
Adjutant	Harry R. Brenneman	Lancaster	Oct. 12, 1864,	
Quartermaster	Freeman P. Bartlett	Warren	Feb. 4, 1865,	
Commissary	Henry D. Frazier	Allegheny	Feb. 20, 1865,	
Company A:				
Captain	Henry N. Harrison	Philadelphia	Nov. 8, 1864,	
First Lieutenant	Wm. H. Collings	Do	Nov. 8, 1864,	
Do	John M. Fleming	Armstrong	July 5, 1865,	
Second Lieutenant	George H. Mowrer	Philadelphia	Nov. 8, 1864,	
Do	Samuel M. Smith	Armstrong	July 5, 1865,	
Company B:				
Captain	Thomas P. Walker	Fayette	June 6, 1865,	
First Lieutenant	John H. Byers	Do	Feb. 4, 1865,	Honorably discharged June 5, 1865
Do	Joseph A. Ripple	Lawrence	June 6, 1865,	
Second Lieutenant	Thomas P. Walker	Fayette	Feb. 4, 1865,	To Captain
Do	Benj. J. Townsend	Beaver	June 6, 1865,	
Company C:				
Captain	Henry B. Hagy	Allegheny	June 29, 1865,	
Company D:				
Captain	Wm. H. Wakefield	Allegheny	Mar. 8, 1865,	Honorably discharged June 9, 1865
Do	Matthew M. Wilson	Do	June 6, 1865,	

EXECUTIVE MILITARY DEPARTMENT.

First Lieutenant....	Matthew M. Wilson....	Allegheny.........	Mar. 8, 1865,	To Captain...............
Second Lieutenant..	Samuel S. Pollock.......	Clarion............	Mar. 8, 1865,	
Company E:				
First Lieutenant....	Andrew G. Hague........	Fayette............	May 20, 1865,	Hon. discharged as 2d Lieut. June 7, 1865.
Second Lieutenant..	Wartman Davis...........	Greene.............	May 20, 1865,	
Company F:				
Captain...............	Jos. S. Schoonmaker....	Allegheny.........	Oct. 24, 1864,	
Do......................	George H. North.........	Philadelphia......	Feb. 4, 1865,	
First Lieutenant....	John S. Nesmith.........	Fayette............	Oct. 24, 1864,	
Second Lieutenant..	Nelson E. Huntsman ...	Allegheny.........	Oct. 24, 1864,	
Company G:				
Captain...............	William W. Murphy....	Westmoreland ..	June 7, 1865,	
First Lieutenant....	Evan R. Jones.............	Allegheny.........	June 7, 1865,	
Second Lieutenant..	James J. Mears...........	......Do	June 6, 1865,	
Company H:				
First Lieutenant....	Henry M'Murray........	Washington	June 5, 1865,	
Second Lieutenant..	James B. Johnston......	......Do.............	June 6, 1865,	
Company I:				
Captain...............	George H. Wetmer......	Warren............	Dec. 18, 1864,	
First Lieutenant....	Charles C. Holliday....	Erie.................	Dec. 18, 1864,	To Quartermaster.........
Second Lieutenant..	Freeman P. Bartlett....	Warren............	Dec. 18, 1864,	
Do......................	Edgar Pierce	Erie.................	Mar. 8, 1865,	
Company K:				
Captain...............	James L. Kelley	Armstrong	May 16, 1865,	
First Lieutenant....	James L. Kelley	......Do	Nov. 8, 1864,	To Captain...............
Do......................	J. B. M'Laughlin ,.......	......Do	May 16, 1865,	
Second Lieutenant..	J. B. M'Laughlin ,.......	......Do	Nov. 8, 1864,	To First Lieutenant.

ONE HUNDRED AND FIFTY-NINTH REGIMENT—Continued.

RANK.	NAME.	CO. OF RESIDENCE.	DATE OF RANK.	REMARKS.
Company L:				
Captain	Samuel D. Hazlett	Butler	April 30, 1865,	
First Lieutenant	David C. Beale	Westmoreland	April 30, 1865,	
Second Lieutenant	Robert Wilson	Do	April 30, 1865,	
Company M:				
Captain	Matthew M. Wilson	Armstrong	Sept. 19, 1864,	
First Lieutenant	Jake Shoop	Do	Sept. 19, 1864,	
Do	David B. Coulter	Do	April 30, 1865,	
Second Lieutenant	David B. Coulter	Do	Sept. 19, 1864,	To First Lieutenant
Do	Milton M'Cormick	Do	April 30, 1865,	

OFFICERS OF THE 160th REGIMENT, FIFTEENTH CAVALRY.

RANK.	NAME.	CO. OF RESIDENCE.	DATE OF RANK.	REMARKS.
Lieutenant Colonel.	Charles M. Betts	Bucks	Jan. 20, 1865,	
Major	George E. Gourand	Chester	Dec. 1, 1864,	Not mustered.
Do	William Wagner	Philadelphia	Jan. 20, 1865,	
Do	Abram B. Garner	Do	Feb. 15, 1865,	
Do	Henry M'Allister, Jr	Delaware	June 1, 1865,	
Adjutant	Josiah C. Reiff	Philadelphia	Jan. 20, 1865,	
Company A:				
Captain	James H. Lloyd	Allegheny	June 21, 1865,	
First Lieutenant	W. W. Borst	Huntingdon	June 21, 1865,	
Second Lieutenant	Arthur P. Lyon	Beaver	Dec. 28, 1864,	Killed by Rebel General Lyon.
Do	Eben Allison	Allegheny	Mar. 15, 1865,	
Do	Henry H. Vance	Allegheny	June 21, 1865,	
Company B:				
Captain	Geo. W. Hildebrand	Adams	Jan. 20, 1865,	
First Lieutenant	John F. Conaway	Philadelphia	Feb 15, 1865,	
Second Lieutenant	Henry H. Vance	Allegheny	May 29, 1865,	To Second Lieutenant Company A
Company C:				
Second Lieutenant	George M. Petty	Allegheny	May 29, 1865,	
Company D:				
Second Lieutenant	William F. Pattison	Philadelphia	Mar. 15, 1865,	
Company E:				
Second Lieutenant	John Burton	Bucks	Mar. 15, 1865,	

ONE HUNDRED AND SIXTIETH REGIMENT—Continued.

RANK.	NAME.	CO. OF RESIDENCE.	DATE OF RANK.	REMARKS.
Company F:				
Second Lieutenant...	John K. Marshall......	Adams...........	May 29, 1865,	
Company G:				
Captain..............	Anthony Taylor.........	Bucks...........	June 1, 1865,	
Second Lieutenant..	Edward Middleton......	Delaware........	May 29, 1865,	
Company H:				
Captain..............	Henry K. Weand	Montgomery......	Feb. 20, 1865,	
First Lieutenant....	Josiah C. Reiff..........	Philadelphia.....	Dec. 1, 1864,	
Do	Theodore M. Ramsey ..	Montgomery......	Jan. 20, 1865,	To Adjutant....
Second Lieutenant..	George S. Yerkes.......	Philadelphia.....	May 29, 1865,	
Company I:				
Second Lieutenant.	Selden L. Wilson.........	Washington......	May 29, 1865,	
Company K:				
Captain..............	Charles E. Scheide......	Philadelphia.....	Jan. 20, 1865,	
Second Lieutenant..	Michael M. Musser......	Centre...........	May 29, 1865,	
Company L:				
Second Lieutenant..	A. B. Coleman...........	....	Mar. 15, 1865,	
Company M:				
First Lieutenant....	David R. Connard.......	....	Feb. 20, 1865,	
Second Lieutenant..	W. W. Borst.............	Huntingdon......	May 29, 1865,	

OFFICERS OF THE 161st REGIMENT, SIXTEENTH CAVALRY.

RANK.	NAME.	CO. OF RESIDENCE.	DATE OF RANK.	REMARKS.
Major	Adam J. Snyder	Franklin	Mar. 8, 1865	
Do	Robert W. M'Dowell	Fayette	May 18, 1865	
Chaplain	D. S. Truckanmiller	Columbia	Mar. 7, 1865	
Company B:				
Captain	George W. Brooks	Fayette	May 18, 1865	
First Lieutenant	William M. Everhart	Centre	May 18, 1865	
Second Lieutenant	William F. Walters	Fayette	May 18, 1865	
Company C:				
Second Lieutenant	A. M. Baccus	Erie	April 4, 1865	
Company D:				
Captain	Erastus T. Robins	Bradford	Dec. 1, 1864	
First Lieutenant	Erastus T. Robins	Do	Oct. 28, 1864	To Captain
Do	Wm. H. Beardsley	Tioga	Dec. 1, 1864	
Do	John H. Morrison	Juniata	April 4, 1865	
Second Lieutenant	Wm. H. Beardsley	Tioga	Oct. 28, 1864	To First Lieutenant
Do	John H. Morrison	Juniata	Feb. 13, 1865	To First Lieutenant
Do	E. G. Kingsley	Do	April 4, 1865	
Company E:				
Captain	Daniel E. Swank	Columbia	Mar. 27, 1865	
First Lieutenant	Russel R. Pealer	Do	Mar. 27, 1865	
Second Lieutenant	Aaron Andrews	Do	Mar. 27, 1865	

ONE HUNDRED AND SIXTY-FIRST REGIMENT—Continued.

RANK.	NAME.	CO. OF RESIDENCE.	DATE OF RANK.	REMARKS.
Company F :				
Captain	Samuel H. Brown	Juniata	May 23, 1865,	
First Lieutenant	Abel D. Hilborn	Do	May 23, 1865,	
Second Lieutenant	Andrew Tyson	Do	May 23, 1865,	
Company G :				
Second Lieutenant	Henry Schively	Philadelphia	Mar. 26, 1865,	
Company H :				
Captain	Solomon B. Barnes	Franklin	Mar. 8, 1865,	
First Lieutenant	Samuel B. Peters	Do	Mar. 8, 1865,	
Second Lieutenant	Samuel B. Peters	Do	Nov. 8, 1864,	To First Lieutenant
Do	Jerome Coble	Do	Mar. 27, 1865,	
Company I :				
Second Lieutenant	George D. Beecher	Tioga	Dec. 13, 1864,	
Company K :				
Second Lieutenant	John Newton Minton	Washington	Dec. 2, 1864,	
Company L :				
Second Lieutenant	Samuel H. Sanders	Northumberland,	July 24, 1864,	

EXECUTIVE MILITARY DEPARTMENT. 187

OFFICERS OF THE 162d REGIMENT, SEVENTEENTH CAVALRY.

RANK.	NAME.	CO. OF RESIDENCE.	DATE OF RANK.	REMARKS.
Colonel	J. Q. Anderson	Beaver	Dec. 18, 1864,	
Lieutenant Colonel	Col. Durland	Wayne	Dec. 18, 1864,	
Major	Luther B. Kurtz	Franklin	Aug. 10, 1864,	
Do	William Thompson	Schuylkill	Dec. 18, 1864,	
Chaplain	R. S. Morton	Beaver	Feb. 19, 1865,	
Company A:				
First Lieutenant	Brice S. Ramsay	Beaver	Sept. 25, 1864,	
Second Lieutenant	David G. Bruce	......Do	Sept. 25, 1864,	
Company C:				
Second Lieutenant	John L. Bechtle	Lancaster	Nov. 1, 1864,	
Company D:				
Second Lieutenant	Stanley Mitchell	Bradford	Nov. 1, 1864,	
Company E:				
First Lieutenant	Levi Loux	Lebanon	July 16, 1864,	
Second Lieutenant	Enos P. Jeffries	Montgomery	July 16, 1864,	
Company F:				
First Lieutenant	John H. Paul	Cumberland	Dec. 23, 1864,	
Second Lieutenant	James B. Green	......Do	Dec. 23, 1864,	
Company G:				
Captain	David Snively	Franklin	Feb. 8, 1865,	
First Lieutenant	H. G. Bonebrake	......Do	Feb. 8, 1865,	

ONE HUNDRED AND SIXTY-SECOND REGIMENT—Continued.

RANK.	NAME.	CO. OF RESIDENCE.	DATE OF RANK.	REMARKS.
Second Lieutenant.	H. G. Bonebrake	Franklin	Nov. 1, 1864,	To First Lieutenant.
Do	Jacob Potter	...Do	Feb. 8, 1865,	
Company H:				
Captain	William J. Allen	Northumberland,	Feb. 8, 1865,	
First Lieutenant	Philip Luckner	...Do	Feb. 8, 1865,	
Second Lieutenant.	Philip Luckner	...Do	Jan. 7, 1865,	To First Lieutenant.
Do	J. E. Fertig	...Do	Feb. 8, 1865,	
Company I:				
Captain	U. R. Reinhold	Lebanon	Jan. 14, 1865,	
First Lieutenant	John Winchester	Perry	Jan. 17, 1865,	
Company M:				
Captain	Frederick J. Skeels	Wayne	April 2, 1865,	
Second Lieutenant.	James Brannon	...Do	April 2, 1865,	

EXECUTIVE MILITARY DEPARTMENT.

RANK.	NAME.	CO. OF RESIDENCE.	DATE OF RANK.	REMARKS.
Colonel............	Theo. F. Rodenbaugh..	Northampton.....	Jan. 1, 1865,	....
Lieutenant Colonel.	John W. Phillips.........	Crawford.........	Mar. 1, 1865,	....
Adjutant.............	Samuel Smith.............	Philadelphia.....	April 14, 1865,	....
Company A:				
Second Lieutenant..	William Scott.............	Greene.............	Dec. 1, 1864,	....
Company B:				
Captain.............	Thomas J. Grier..........	Somerset..........	Feb. 7, 1865,	....
First Lieutenant...	James M'Kay.............	Crawford..........	Feb. 7, 1865,	....
Second Lieutenant..	Charles A. Clark........	......Do...........	Feb. 7, 1865,	....
Company C:				
First Lieutenant....	Charles Edwards........	Luzerne...........	May 16, 1865,	....
Company D:				
Second Lieutenant..	Francis M. Magee.......	Crawford..........	Dec. 1, 1864,	....
Company E:				
First Lieutenant....	Theodore Jackman.....	Allegheny........	Dec. 1, 1864,	....
Second Lieutenant..	William P. Seal..........	Dauphin...........	Dec. 1, 1864,	....
Company F:				
Captain.............	James Moffit.............	Fayette............	Oct. 3, 1864,	....
First Lieutenant....	William A. Young......	Washington......	Oct. 3, 1864,	....

ONE HUNDRED AND SIXTY-THIRD REGIMENT—Continued.

RANK.	NAME.	CO. OF RESIDENCE.	DATE OF RANK.	REMARKS.
Company G:				
Captain............	Benj. F. Herrington....	Greene............	April 8, 1865,	....
First Lieutenant.....	John Rogers............	....Do	April 8, 1865,	....
Company K:				
First Lieutenant.....	W. A. Rogers	Cambria...........	May 15, 1865,	....
Company L:				
Captain............	Henry C. Potter	Philadelphia......	April 14, 1865,	....
Company M:				
Captain............	Enos J. Pennypacker...	Philadelphia.....	Dec. 8, 1862,	....

OFFICERS OF THE 180th REGIMENT, NINETEENTH CAVALRY.

RANK.	NAME.	CO. OF RESIDENCE.	DATE OF RANK.	REMARKS.
Lieutenant Colonel.	Frank Reeder............	Northampton....	Jan. 26, 1865,	
Major..................	Charles F. Huston......	Centre.............	July 1, 1864,	
Adjutant.............	Roland C. Allen.........	Philadelphia.....	July 12, 1865,	
Company A:				
Second Lieutenant..	Charles P. Holahan.....	Philadelphia.....	Jan. 26, 1865,	
Company B:				
Captain................	Maurice E. Fagan.......	Philadelphia.....	Jan. 26, 1865,	
Second Lieutenant..	Louis V. Boursch........	......Do	Jan. 26, 1865,	
Company C:				
Captain................	Norman M. Smith.......	Philadelphia.....	Jan. 26, 1865,	
Second Lieutenant...	James C. Pope...........	......Do	Jan. 26, 1865,	
Company D:				
Captain...............	Joseph C. Castle	Philadelphia.....	Feb. 19, 1865,	
First Lieutenant	John Dunlap.............	......Do	Jan. 26, 1865,	
Second Lieutenant..	Edward P. M'Carthy...	......Do	Jan. 26, 1865,	
Company E:				
Second Lieutenant..	Joseph H. Watson......	Philadelphia.....	Jan. 26, 1865,	
Company F:				
First Lieutenant	James Blackstone.......	Philadelphia.....	Jan. 26, 1865,	
Second Lieutenant..	Joseph H. Bond.........	......Do	Jan. 26, 1865,	

OFFICERS OF THE 181st REGIMENT, TWENTIETH CAVALRY.

RANK.	NAME.	CO. OF RESIDENCE.	DATE OF RANK.	REMARKS.
Colonel...............	Gabriel Middleton.......	Philadelphia.....	Jan. 19, 1865,	....
LieutenantColonel.	Robert B. Douglass......	......Do	Feb. 25, 1865,	....
Major.................	Michael B. Strickler....	......Do	Feb. 25, 1865,	....
Do	Samuel Comfort..........	......Do	Feb. 25, 1865,	....
Adjutant.............	Thomas A. Davis.........	......Do	Feb. 25, 1865,	....
Quartermaster.......	George W. Eachus........	Delaware.........	April 1, 1865,	....
Company A:				
Captain..............	John W. Macklin.........	Cumberland.....	April 1, 1865,	....
First Lieutenant...	J. W. Armstrong	......Do	April 1, 1865,	....
Second Lieutenant.	James I. Macklin........	......Do	April 1, 1865,	....
Company B:				
Captain..............	George Ostott............	....	April 1, 1865,	....
First Lieutenant...	William L. Spangler...	Huntingdon	April 1, 1865,	....
Second Lieutenant.	George Ostott............	....	Oct. 4, 1864,	To Captain.......
Company F:				
Captain..............	Samuel S. Ely............	Bucks.............	Feb. 25, 1865,	....
First Lieutenant...	Evan E. Bartleson.......	Delaware.........	April 23, 1865,	....
Second Lieutenant.	Evan E. Bartleson.......	....Do	April 1, 1865,	To First Lieutenant.......
Do	Frank Buckman..........	Bucks.............	April 23, 1865,	....
Company G:				
Captain..............	Benjamin H. Sweeny...	Chester...........	Sept. 28, 1864,	....

EXECUTIVE MILITARY DEPARTMENT. 193

Company H:				
Second Lieutenant..	Andrew Jackson........	Bucks........	April 1, 1865,	....
Company I:				
Captain.................	Horace B. Haldeman....	Philadelphia......	Feb. 25, 1865,	....
First Lieutenant.....	Horace B. Haldeman....	....Do............	Sept. 22, 1864,	To Captain............
Second Lieutenant...	Charles F. Wright.......	Lancaster.........	Nov. 20, 1864,	....
Company K:				
Second Lieutenant...	Knight B. Kannegy.....	....	Oct. 22, 1864,	....
Company L:				
First Lieutenant.....	Henry Lebo.............	Dauphin...........	Feb. 25, 1865,	....
Do......................	Charles F. Miller........	Philadelphia......	April 23, 1865,	....
Second Lieutenant..	Wash'n L. Watkinson...	.....Do............	April 23, 1865,	....
Company M:				
First Lieutenant.....	Alfred Brinton...........	Chester............	Sept. 28, 1864,	....
Second Lieutenant...	John H. Babb............	....Do.............	Sept. 28, 1864,	....
Do......................	Payne A Gould...........	....Do.............	April 23, 1865,	....

13 MILITARY DEPART.

OFFICERS OF THE 182d REGIMENT, TWENTY-FIRST CAVALRY.

RANK.	NAME.	CO. OF RESIDENCE.	DATE OF RANK.	REMARKS.
Colonel	Oliver B. Knowles	Philadelphia	Nov. 5, 1864,	
Major	Charles F. Gillies	....Do	Oct. 5, 1864,	
Adjutant	Henry B. Kindig	Franklin	May 17, 1865,	
Commissary	William H. Pfoutz	....Do	April 5, 1865,	Hon. disch'd as 1st Lieut. May 15, 1865.
Company A:				
Captain	Hugh W. M'Call	York	Nov. 18, 1863,	
First Lieutenant	James T. Long	Franklin	July 25, 1865,	
Second Lieutenant	Samuel M. Manifold	York	July 25, 1865,	
Company B:				
Captain	Isaac Bucher	Adams	June 9, 1865,	
First Lieutenant	John Q. A. Young	...Do	June 9, 1865,	
Second Lieutenant	La Fayette Brenizer	Cumberland	June 9, 1865,	
Company C:				
Captain	Wilson Strickler	Lancaster	Nov. 18, 1864,	
Do	Charles E. Pettis	Warren	June 9, 1865,	
First Lieutenant	Charles E. Pettis	....Do	Nov. 18, 1864,	To Captain.
Do	Henry H. M'Laughlin	Mifflin	June 9, 1865,	
Second Lieutenant	Henry H. M'Laughlin	....Do	Nov. 18, 1864,	To First Lieutenant.
Do	William O. Guier	Luzerne	June 9, 1865,	
Company D:				
Captain	James C. Patton	Franklin	May 21, 1865,	
First Lieutenant	D. L. Pisle	....Do	May 21, 1865,	
Second Lieutenant	M'Farland Campbell	....Do	May 21, 1865,	

Company E:			
Captain	M. V. B. Coho	Schuylkill	June 9, 1865,
First Lieutenant	Thomas A. Blanchard	Warren	June 9, 1865,
Second Lieutenant	George Roth	Franklin	June 9, 1865,
Company F:			
Captain	Samuel Henry	Cambria	May 17, 1865,
First Lieutenant	Henry C. Teeter	Do	Oct. 6, 1864,
Second Lieutenant	J. Henry Treice	Indiana	Oct. 6, 1864,
Do	Wm. H. Slater	Cambria	July 25, 1865,
Company G:			
First Lieutenant	Wm. Chandler	Lancaster	Mar. 21, 1865,
Second Lieutenant	Ernest D. Reynolds	Do	Mar. 21, 1865,
Company H:			
First Lieutenant	John Lamond	Schuylkill	April 8, 1865,
Second Lieutenant	R. Sherman Lerch	Do	April 8, 1865,
Company I:			
First Lieutenant	William Keiffer	Lancaster	May 21, 1865,
Company K:			
First Lieutenant	George W. Kennedy	Franklin	June 9, 1865,
Second Lieutenant	Samuel Palmer	Do	June 9, 1865,
Company L:			
First Lieutenant	Fred. W. Shinafield	Franklin	July 25, 1865,
Second Lieutenant	George H. Harmony	Do	July 25, 1865,
Company M:			
Captain	John A. Devers	Schuylkill	April 23, 1865,
First Lieutenant	Abraham Myers	Chester	April 23, 1865,
Second Lieutenant	Joshua Haines	Philadelphia	April 23, 1865,

OFFICERS OF THE 183d REGIMENT, INFANTRY

RANK.	NAME.	CO. OF RESIDENCE.	DATE OF RANK.	REMARKS.
Major............	Horace P. Egbert.......	Philadelphia.....	Oct. 7, 1864,	....
Company A :				
Captain...........	Samuel M'Nutt..........	Philadelphia......	Oct. 7, 1864,	....
First Lieutenant....	Edward L. M'Gowan...	......Do.............	Oct. 7, 1864,	....
Second Lieutenant..	Edward L. M'Gowan...	......Do.............	Feb. 12, 1865,	To First Lieutenant.....
Do	Colin M. Beale.........	......Do.............	July 10, 1865,	....
Company B :				
First Lieutenant....	Charles H. Hamm......	Philadelphia.....	Sept. 8, 1864,	....
Do	Robert G. Caterson.....	......Do.............	May 20, 1865,	....
Second Lieutenant..	Robert G. Caterson.....	......Do.............	Sept. 8, 1864,	To First Lieutenant.....
Do	Charles Miller	......Do.............	May 20, 1865,	....
Company C :				
Captain............	George T. Elliott........	Philadelphia.....	Feb. 6, 1865,	....
First Lieutenant....	Benjamin F. Jones	......Do.............	Feb. 6, 1865,	....
Second Lieutenant..	Samuel S. Hawk........	......Do.............	Mar. 28, 1865,	....
Company D :				
Captain.	Michael Hartzell........	Philadelphia....	Aug. 20, 1864,	....
First Lieutenant....	Bennett B. Lynch........	......Do	Aug. 20, 1864,	....
Second Lieutenant..	John A. White..........	......Do	July 10, 1865,	....
Company E :				
First Lieutenant....	Charles H. Crawford..	Philadelphia......	Oct. 9, 1864,	Hon. discharged as Second Lieut., to date [May 15, 1865.
Second Lieutenant..	Charles Lukowitz.......	Schuylkill.........	July 10, 1865,	....

EXECUTIVE MILITARY DEPARTMENT. 197

Company F:				
First Lieutenant.....	William Edggar...........	Philadelphia......	Dec. 17, 1864,	
Second Lieutenant. .	John J. Weiser.......	....Do.....	Dec. 17, 1864,	
Company G:				
First Lieutenant.....	George T. Elliott........	Philadelphia.....	Aug. 10, 1864,	To Captain Company C......
Do	Theodore Loveaire ..	......Do	Feb. 6, 1865,	
Second Lieutenant. .	Theodore Loveaire	......Do	Dec. 17, 1864,	To First Lieutenant......
Do	Michael F. Donahoe......	......Do	July 10, 1865,	
Company H:				
Captain.............	Robert M'Lean	Philadelphia......	April 30, 1865,	
First Lieutenant	Francis M. Elliott.........	....Do	May 31, 1865,	
Second Lieutenant. .	Jacob S. Stott	Chester	July 10, 1865,	
Company I:				
First Lieutenant.....	William P. Pontzler......	Philadelphia.....	Jan 5, 1865,	
Second Lieutenant. .	William P. Pontzler.......	....Do	July 20, 1864,	To First Lieutenant......
Do	Michael F. Barr...........	....Do	July 10, 1865,	
Company K:				
First Lieutenant.....	Benj. H. M'Gowan.......	Philadelphia.....	Nov. 29, 1864,	
Second Lieutenant .	James Park...............	....Do	July 10, 1865,	

OFFICERS OF THE 184th REGIMENT, INFANTRY.

RANK.	NAME.	CO. OF RESIDENCE.	DATE OF RANK.	REMARKS.
Adjutant............	Wilson L. Plowman....	Blair...............	May 16, 1865,	....
Company A:				
Second Lieutenant..	Barton C. Smith	Bedford.............	June 26, 1865,	....
Company B:				
First Lieutenant	Adam Hand............	Venango	Nov. 1, 1864,	Discharged May 29, 1865.....
Do................	Thomas S. Anderson....	....	June 26, 1865,	....
Second Lieutenant..	Daniel H. Hinkels.......	Philadelphia......	June 26, 1865,	....
Company C:				
First Lieutenant.....	Michael Stover..........	Centre.............	April 14, 1865,	....
Second Lieutenant..	Thomas M. Ditty........	Dauphin..........	April 14, 1865,	....
Company E:				
First Lieutenant....	Hugh T. Harpham	Centre.............	Jan. 2, 1865,	....
Second Lieutenant..	Abner H. Rohrer........	Dauphin..........	June 26, 1865,	....
Company F:				
First Lieutenant....	Henry W. Benfer........	Snyder............	Dec. 13, 1864,	....
Second Lieutenant..	Samuel K. Hoot.........	...Do..	Dec. 13, 1864,	....
Company G:				
Second Lieutenant..	Alexander T. Barnes ...	York...............	June 26, 1865,	....
Company H:				
First Lieutenant.....	Samuel O. M'Curdy....	Union.............	Feb. 1, 1865,	....

EXECUTIVE MILITARY DEPARTMENT.

Second Lieutenant..	John L. Jacobs..........	Lancaster.........	Feb. 1, 1865,
Company I :			
First Lieutenant.....	Paul H. Knopp...........	Snyder........	Jan. 12, 1865,
Second Lieutenant..	Charles H. Haus	Union...........	Jan. 12, 1865,
Company K :			
First Lieutenant.....	Philip L. Houck..........	Adams...........	Feb. 1, 1865,
Second Lieutenant...	Adam B. Black...........	....Do.............	Feb. 1, 1865,

OFFICERS OF THE 185th REGIMENT, TWENTY-SECOND CAVALRY.

RANK.	NAME.	CO. OF RESIDENCE.	DATE OF RANK.	REMARKS.
Company B:				
Captain............	William E. Griffith.......	Washington......	Mar. 3, 1865,	....
First Lieutenant....	John B. Henderson......	Do	Mar. 3, 1865,	....
Second Lieutenant..	John B. Henderson......	Do	Dec. 25, 1864,	To First Lieutenant.....
Do	Joshua B. Deems........	Do	Mar. 3, 1865,	....
Company D:				
Captain............	Felix Boyle	Washington	Mar. 19, 1865,	....
First Lieutenant....	James B. Gibson	Do	Mar. 19, 1865,	....
Second Lieutenant..	Clinton Temple..........	Do........	Mar. 19, 1865,	....
Company E:				
First Lieutenant....	Benjamin F. Hassan....	Washington	May 17, 1865,	....
Second Lieutenant..	William Hedge..........	Do........	May 17, 1865,	....
Company F:				
First Lieutenant....	Jefferson G. Van Gilder,	....	Dec. 22, 1864,	....
Second Lieutenant..	James G. Hubbs........	....	Dec 22, 1864,	....
Do.............	William H. Frost........	Greene	May 31, 1865,	....
Company H:				
First Lieutenant....	Washington Morrison...	Adams......	Mar. 3, 1865,	....
Second Lieutenant..	Washington Morrison...	Do......	Dec. 25, 1864,	To First Lieutenant.....
Do.............	David G. Ganoe.........	Blair......	Mar. 3, 1865,	....
Company I:				
Captain............	C. S. Derland..........	Blair......	May 31, 1865,	....

EXECUTIVE MILITARY DEPARTMENT. 201

Second Lieutenant.	Robert A. Laird.........	Juniata.........	May 31, 1865,
Company K:			
First Lieutenant.....	Wilber F. Sharrer.......	Huntingdon	June 13, 1865,
Second Lieutenant.	David P. Kinkead......	......Do	June 13, 1865,
Company L:			
Second Lieutenant.	Joseph Burk.............	Franklin.........	May 31, 1865,
Company M:			
Second Lieutenant.	George N. Young.......	Bedford.........	June 13, 1865,

OFFICERS OF THE 187th REGIMENT, INFANTRY.

RANK.	NAME.	CO. OF RESIDENCE.	DATE OF RANK.	REMARKS.
Colonel	John E. Parsons	Dauphin	May 1, 1865	
Lieutenant Colonel	John E. Parsons	Do	Jan. 27, 1865	To Colonel
Do	Joseph A. Ege	Cumberland	May 1, 1865	
Major	David Z. Seip	York	May 1, 1865	
Company A:				
Captain	Robert Young	Tioga	Mar. 10, 1865	
First Lieutenant	Timothy B. Culver	Do	Mar. 10, 1865	
Second Lieutenant	Timothy B. Culver	Do	Sept. 3, 1864	To First Lieutenant
Do	William A. Stone	Do	Mar. 10, 1865	
Company B:				
Captain	Samuel J. Adams	York	May 1, 1865	
First Lieutenant	Wm. W. Torbert	Do	May 1, 1865	
Second Lieutenant	Samuel C. Ilgenfritz	Do	May 1, 1865	
Company D:				
Captain	John E. Frymier	Cumberland	May 1, 1865	
First Lieutenant	John S. Gore	Philadelphia	May 1, 1865	
Second Lieutenant	Frank Best	Franklin	May 1, 1865	
Company E:				
Captain	Frederick B. Argue	Philadelphia	April 18, 1865	
First Lieutenant	James Slemmer	Do	April 18, 1865	
Second Lieutenant	Edward Steele	Do	April 18, 1865	

EXECUTIVE MILITARY DEPARTMENT.

Company F:			
First Lieutenant	Paul E. Cowper	Philadelphia	June 6, 1865,
Second Lieutenant	Gideon W. Myers	......Do	June 6, 1865,
Company H:			
First Lieutenant	Charles F. Fennerstein	Luzerne	May 6, 1865,
Second Lieutenant	Charles F. Fennerstein	......Do	Mar. 1, 1865, To First Lieutenant
Do	Porter Squires	Wyoming	May 6, 1865,
Company I:			
Captain	Ransford B. Webb	Tioga	Sept. 24, 1864,
First Lieutenant	Monroe P. Crosby		Sept. 24, 1864,
Second Lieutenant	W. E. Zinn		Feb. 24, 1865,
Company K:			
Second Lieutenant	George S. Walker	Montour	Dec. 19, 1864,

OFFICERS OF THE 188th REGIMENT, INFANTRY.

RANK.	NAME.	CO. OF RESIDENCE.	DATE OF RANK.	REMARKS.
Colonel.............	John G. Gregg............	....	May 1, 1865,	....
Lieutenant Colonel..	John G. Gregg............	....	Mar. 28, 1865,	To Colonel........
Do	Samuel J. Given	Philadelphia.....	May 1, 1865,	....
Major	John G. Gregg............	....	July 17, 1864,	To Lieutenant Colonel...
Do	James Geiser.............	Philadelphia.....	May 1, 1865,	....
Quartermaster......	Lot I. Leech..............	Centre...........	Dec. 23, 1864,	....
Company A:				
Captain............	Hannam Gray.............	Luzerne..........	Dec. 2, 1864,	....
Do	Sylvester J. Hinds........	..Do.............	July 8, 1865,	....
First Lieutenant....	Sylvester J. Hinds........	..Do.............	Feb. 1, 1865,	To Captain........
Do	Philander K. Potter	..Do.............	July 8, 1865,	....
Company B:				
Captain............	Frederick A. Reen........	....	Sept. 25, 1864,	....
First Lieutenant....	Frederick Winter.........	Centre...........	Sept. 25, 1864,	....
Do	Samuel M. Shuler.........	Perry............	June 8, 1865,	....
Company C:				
Captain............	William P. Young.........	Philadelphia.....	June 2, 1864,	....
Do	Louis A. Uhl	..Do.............	Dec. 23, 1864,	To Captain........
First Lieutenant....	Louis A. Uhl	..Do.............	June 2, 1864,	To Captain........
Do	Adam C. Bartholow.......	..Do.............	Dec. 23, 1864,	....
Do	John Davis................	Chester..........	June 20, 1865,	....
Company D:				
Captain............	James Geisler............	....	July 17, 1864,	....
First Lieutenant....	Harry J. Cogan...........	Huntingdon......	July 17, 1864,	....

EXECUTIVE MILITARY DEPARTMENT. 205

Captain	Abijah S. Jackson	Philadelphia	Dec. 1, 1864		
Do	George Geiser	Blair	May 1, 1865		
Do	Joseph A. Chambers	Allegheny	May 12, 1865		
First Lieutenant	Alexander Masters	Philadelphia	Dec. 1, 1864		
Do	Robert Williams	Do	May 12, 1865		
Do	Abraham S. Diel		July 8, 1865		
First Lieutenant	John Austin	Delaware	Oct. 1, 1864		
Do	Edward L. M'Cluen	Chester	May 1, 1865		
Company G:					
Captain	George H. Borger	Bedford	Dec. 16, 1864		
First Lieutenant	Joseph M. Barkman		Dec. 16, 1864		
Do	David W. Ball	Philadelphia	July 1, 1865		
Company H:					
Captain	John Carson	Allegheny	Dec. 1, 1864		
Do	Joseph Elliot		Dec. 23, 1864		
First Lieutenant	Joseph Elliot	Do	Dec. 1, 1864	To Captain.	
Do	Henry P. Cooper	Philadelphia	Dec. 23, 1864		
Company I:					
Captain	John W. Keough		Dec. 1, 1864		
First Lieutenant	Henry Burbank		Dec. 1, 1864		
Do	John W. Smith	Philadelphia	June 17, 1865		
Company K:					
Captain	Henry Fox	York	May 1, 1865		
First Lieutenant	James Boone	Allegheny	May 1, 1865		

OFFICERS OF THE 190th REGIMENT, INFANTRY.

RANK.	NAME.	CO. OF RESIDENCE.	DATE OF RANK.	REMARKS.
Company I:				
Captain............	Wm. E. Murray.........	Northampton....	Dec. 4, 1864,	....
First Lieutenant.....	Wm. C. Coleman.........	....	Dec. 4, 1864,	....

OFFICERS OF THE 191st REGIMENT, INFANTRY.

RANK.	NAME.	CO. OF RESIDENCE.	DATE OF RANK.	REMARKS.
Lieutenant Colonel..	Milton Weidler...........	Lancaster.........	Mar. 1, 1865,	
Chaplain...................	Walter R. Whitney......	Bedford.............	April 24, 1865,	
Company A:				
Captain................	Andrew M. R. Storrie..	Philadelphia.....	Sept. 5, 1864,	
First Lieutenant....	Henry Mullen...............	Lancaster.........	June 8, 1864,	
Company B:				
Captain................	John L. Benzon............	Philadelphia.....	Dec. 1, 1864,	
Company D:				
Captain................	Richard H. Walk..........	Centre..............	June 17, 1864,	
First Lieutenant....	Livingston Bogart........	Tioga................	June 17, 1864,	
Company E:				
First Lieutenant....	George W. Belcher.......		Nov. 1, 1864,	
Second Lieutenant..	Isaac H. Ball.................		Nov. 1, 1864,	
Company F:				
Captain................	Thomas H. Abbott.......	Philadelphia.....	Sept. 5, 1864,	
First Lieutenant....	John Flynn....................	Bradford...........	Sept. 5, 1864,	
Company K:				
First Lieutenant....	Wm. M. Slater..............	Mercer..............	Nov. 22, 1864,	

OFFICERS OF THE 192d REGIMENT, INFANTRY.

RANK.	NAME.	CO. OF RESIDENCE.	DATE OF RANK.	REMARKS.
Colonel............	William W. Stewart....	Adams	Mar. 15, 1865,	....
Lieutenant Colonel.	Thomas M'Leester......	Philadelphia.....	Mar. 15, 1865,	....
Major.......	William F. Johnston....	Huntingdon	April 13, 1865,	....
Adjutant............	Alfred Rupert............	Lancaster.....	Mar. 15, 1865,	....
Quartermaster.......	John A. Waggoner......	Cumberland.....	Mar. 15, 1865,	....
Chaplain............	S. S. Richmond............	......Do	April 22, 1865,	....
Company B:				
Captain........	William F. Johnston....	Huntingdon	Feb. 17, 1865,	To Major........
Do.........	Thomas S. Johnston.....	......Do	April 13, 1865,	....
First Lieutenant.....	Thomas S. Johnston.....	......Do	Feb. 17, 1865,	To Captain......
Do.......	Alfred Tyhurst.........	......Do	April 13, 1865,	....
Second Lieutenant.	Alfred Tyhurst...........	......Do.....	Feb. 17, 1865,	To First Lieutenant ......
Do...........	Henry A. Hoffman.....	......Do	April 13, 1865,	....
Company C:				
Captain...........	David Hummell........	Dauphin........	Feb. 16, 1865,	....
First Lieutenant	Joseph T. Hoover......	Cumberland.....	Feb. 16, 1865,	....
Second Lieutenant.	Moses Lyter............	Dauphin........	Feb. 16, 1865,	....
Company D:				
Captain.........	Samuel A. Andrews.....	Blair........	Feb. 21, 1865,	....
First Lieutenant	James Rodgers	...Do	Feb. 21, 1865,	....
Second Lieutenant..	John Suires............	...Do.........	Feb. 21, 1865,	....
Company E:				
Captain............	Adam Erford	Philadelphia......	Mar. 3, 1865,	Discharged May 29, 1865......

EXECUTIVE MILITARY DEPARTMENT.

Captain............	Charles D. Brooks......	Philadelphia.....	May 30, 1865,	....
First Lieutenant....	Charles D. Brooks......	......Do	Mar. 3, 1865,	To Captain............
Do............	Wm J. D. M'Kee......	......Do	May 30, 1865,	....
Second Lieutenant..	Wm J. D. M'Kee......	......Do	Mar. 3, 1865,	To First Lieutenant.....
Do	James L. Rankin.......	......Do	May 30, 1865,	....
Company F:				
Captain............	John Teed............	Berks.........	Mar. 3, 1865,	....
First Lieutenant....	Samuel M. Snyder	......Do	Mar. 3, 1865,	Discharged June 5, 1865...
Do............	James W. Hill........	......Do	June 6, 1865,	....
Second Lieutenant..	James W. Hill........	......Do	Mar. 3, 1865,	To First Lieutenant......
Do............	Philip Carling........	......Do	June 6, 1865,	....
Company G:				
Captain............	Wm. A. Mackin........	Cambria.........	Mar. 1, 1865,	....
First Lieutenant....	Michael A. Keenan......	Lycoming........	Mar. 1, 1865,	....
Second Lieutenant..	Wm M. Douglass......	Carbon........	Mar. 1, 1865,	....
Company H:				
Captain............	Peter S. Bergstresser...	Dauphin.........	Mar. 2, 1865,	....
First Lieutenant....	Jonathan Tobias.......	......Do	Mar. 2, 1865,	....
Second Lieutenant..	Godfrey Sammet.......	......Do	Mar. 2, 1865,	....
Company I:				
Captain............	J. Wilson Hess........	Northumberland,	Mar. 3, 1865,	....
First Lieutenant....	Isaac H. Wagner.......	Union............	Mar. 3, 1865,	....
Second Lieutenant..	Benj. F. Angstadt......	......Do	Mar. 3, 1865,	....
Company K:				
Captain............	Seth S. Richmond......	Cumberland	Mar. 8, 1865,	....
First Lieutenant....	George W. Newman......	Dauphin	Mar. 8, 1865,	....
Second Lieutenant..	John B. Metzgar.......	York............	Mar. 8, 1865,	....

14 MILITARY DEPART.

OFFICERS OF THE 195th REGIMENT, INFANTRY.

RANK.	NAME.	CO. OF RESIDENCE.	DATE OF RANK.	REMARKS.
Colonel...............	Joseph W. Fisher......	Lancaster.........	Feb. 25, 1865,	
Lieutenant Colonel..	William L. Bear.........	......Do	Feb. 25, 1865,	
Major.................	Henry D. Markley......	Berks...............	Dec. 8, 1864,	
Adjutant..............	John A. Willoughby...	Huntingdon	Feb. 25, 1865,	
Quartermaster.......	Hiram Stamm..........	Lancaster.........	Feb. 25, 1865,	
Chaplain..............	Isaac E. Graeff.........	......Do	Mar. 16, 1865,	
Company A:				
Captain...............	Henry D. Markley......	Berks...............	July 16, 1864,	To Major.........
Do	Samuel J. M'Pherson...	Huntingdon	Feb. 25, 1865,	
First Lieutenant ...	Samuel J. M'Pherson...	......Do	July 21, 1864,	To Captain.......
Do	Samuel Parvin...........	Berks...............	Feb. 25, 1865,	
Second Lieutenant..	Samuel Parvin...........	......Do	July 16, 1865,	To First Lieutenant...
Do	Martin Wagner.........	......Do	Feb. 25, 1865,	
Company B:				
Captain...............	James F. Ricksecker ...	Lancaster......	July 17, 1864,	......
First Lieutenant.....	Hiram Stamm.........	......Do	July 17, 1864,	To Quartermaster...
Do	Daniel R. Kepner.......	Dauphin	Feb. 25, 1865,	
Company C:				
Captain...............	Philip L. Sprecher......	Lancaster.........	July 21, 1865,	
First Lieutenant.....	William D. Stauffer.....	......Do	July 21, 1865,	
Second Lieutenant..	George W. Engle........	......Do	Dec. 2, 1864,	
Company D:				
Captain...............	Christian B. Hebble....	Lancaster.........	Feb. 25, 1865,	

EXECUTIVE MILITARY DEPARTMENT. 211.

First Lieutenant....	J. David Miller..........	Lancaster......	Feb. 25, 1865,	
Second Lieutenant..	James Spindler.........	......Do	Feb. 25, 1865,	
Company E :				
Captain............	Jacob F. Barnitz.........	Lancaster......	Feb. 25, 1865,	
First Lieutenant....	James R. Haldeman....	...Do	Feb. 25, 1865,	
Second Lieutenant..	James A. Hinkle......	......Do	Feb. 25, 1865,	
Company F :				
Captain............	John K. Rutter.........	Lancaster......	Feb. 25, 1865,	
First Lieutenant....	John Z. Thomas.........	......Do......	Feb. 25, 1865,	
Second Lieutenant..	Levi D. Shumon.........	......Do	Feb. 25, 1865,	
Company G :				
Captain............	Edwin H. Faust.........	Lancaster......	Feb. 25, 1865,	
First Lieutenant....	George Frazer...........	......Do	Feb. 25, 1865,	
Second Lieutenant..	H. Augustus Kinch......	......Do	Feb. 25, 1865,	
Company H :				
Captain............	Joseph Styre	Lancaster......	Feb. 25, 1865,	Discharged June 5, 1865......
Do...............	William D. Stauffer.....	......Do	July 1, 1865,	
First Lieutenant....	John S. Rodgers.........	......Do	Feb. 25, 1865,	
Second Lieutenant..	Jefferson Galbraith......	......Do	Feb. 25, 1865,	
Company I :				
Captain............	Joseph Umble...........	Lancaster......	Feb. 25, 1865,	
First Lieutenant....	John D Gallagher.......	......Do	Feb. 25, 1865,	
Second Lieutenant..	Henry M. Trout.........	......Do	Feb. 25, 1865,	
Company K :				
Captain............	Don Juan Wallings	Lancaster......	Feb. 25, 1865,	
First Lieutenant....	George W. Caracher.....	......Do	Feb. 25, 1865,	
Second Lieutenant..	Abram G. Landis........	......Do	Feb. 25, 1865,	

OFFICERS OF THE 198th REGIMENT, INFANTRY.

RANK.	NAME.	CO. OF RESIDENCE.	DATE OF RANK.	REMARKS.
Major.............	Powell Stackhouse......	Cambria..........	April 5, 1865,	....
Do	John Stanton.............	Philadelphia......	April 6, 1865,	....
Adjutant........	James Orne...............	......Do	Jan. 15, 1865,	....
Company A:				
Captain...........	Theodore K. Vogel......	Philadelphia......	April 5, 1865,	....
First Lieutenant.....	Jacob Wheeler.............	......Do...........	April 5, 1865,	....
Company B:				
Captain...........	Edwin Bailey......	Philadelphia......	April 5, 1865,	....
First Lieutenant.....	Benjamin Waite...........	......Do...........	April 5, 1865,	....
Company C:				
Captain...........	Thomas Mitchell........	Philadelphia......	Mar. 29, 1865,	....
First Lieutenant.....	Carlton Birch.............	......Do...........	Mar. 29, 1865,	....
Second Lieutenant. .	James F. Milligan........	......Do...........	Mar. 29, 1865,	....
Company D:				
Captain...........	Adam Faust...............	Berks.............	April 2, 1865,	....
First Lieutenant.....	Joseph H. Lutz............	...Do	April 2, 1865,	....
Second Lieutenant. .	Charles Weber.............	......Do...........	April 2, 1865,	....
Company E:				
Second Lieutenant. .	Henry A. Sheaff........	Philadelphia......	Mar. 24, 1865,	....
Company F:				
Captain...........	George C. Fisher.........	Cambria...........	April 6, 1865,	....

EXECUTIVE MILITARY DEPARTMENT. 213

Second Lieutenant....	Jacob M. Fackler.......	....Do.......	April 6, 1865,
Company I:			
First Lieutenant.....	Charles Raisner.........	Philadelphia......	Mar. 31, 1865,
Company L:			
First Lieutenant.....	Charles Seeley.........	Philadelphia......	Feb. 8, 1865,
Second Lieutenant..	James Clark...........	....Do.......	Mar. 10, 1865,
Company M:			
Captain..............	John M. Barclay.......	Chester...........	Mar. 16, 1865,
First Lieutenant....	Mordecai E. Morris....	....Do.......	Mar. 16, 1865,
Second Lieutenant..	Charles F. Caldwell....	Wayne..........	Mar. 16, 1865,
Company O:			
First Lieutenant.....	Charles W. Showaker...	Philadelphia......	Feb. 17, 1865,
Second Lieutenant..	Robert E. Horner.......	....Do.......	Feb. 17, 1865,

OFFICERS OF THE 199th REGIMENT, INFANTRY.

RANK.	NAME.	CO. OF RESIDENCE.	DATE OF RANK.	REMARKS.
Quartermaster	Charles Moss	Philadelphia	Nov. 14, 1864,	
Chaplain	J. B. H. Janeway	Do	Dec. 24, 1864,	
Company A:				
Captain	Samuel Muchler	Luzerne	Feb. 14, 1865,	To Captain Company D
First Lieutenant	Allen L. Hartwell	Philadelphia	Feb. 14, 1865,	To Captain Company D
Do	Price Williams	Do	May 12, 1865,	To First Lieutenant
Second Lieutenant	Price Williams	Do	Feb. 14, 1865,	
Do	William Tricker	Chester	June 8, 1865,	
Company B:				
Second Lieutenant	Frank Ellison	Philadelphia	Jan. 9, 1865,	To First Lieutenant Company G
Do	Peter Ashen	Do	June 8, 1865,	
Company C:				
First Lieutenant	Lighten O. Colvin	Luzerne	Feb. 14, 1865,	
Second Lieutenant	Cyrus J. Willsey	Bradford	June 8, 1865,	
Company D:				
Captain	Allen L. Hartwell	Philadelphia	May 12, 1865,	
First Lieutenant	Francis Sternberg	Do	Feb. 14, 1865,	
Do	George C. Snyder	Do	June 8, 1865,	
Second Lieutenant	James Patton	Do	Feb. 14, 1865,	
Do	Franklin M'Closky	Chester	May 12, 1865,	
Do	Thomas B. Powers	Philadelphia	June 8, 1865,	

Company E:			
Second Lieutenant..	Isaac Croft.............	Wayne....	June 8, 1865,
Company F:			
First Lieutenant....	Robert Andrews........	Crawford...........	Jan. 9, 1865,
Second Lieutenant..	Seneca W. Palmanteer,	.... Do	May 12, 1865,
Company G:			
First Lieutenant....	Frank Ellison...........	Philadelphia.	June 8, 1865,
Company H:			
First Lieutenant....	Oliver Sproul...........	Fayette	Dec. 15, 1864,
Second Lieutenant..	Morris M. M'Candless,	Armstrong.	Mar. 21, 1865,
Company I:			
Captain.	Judson C. Blanchard...	Crawford..........	Jan. 9, 1865,
First Lieutenant....	James Patton...........	Philadelphia......	May 12, 1865,
Second Lieutenant..	Samuel W. Debolt......	Lycoming..........	May 12, 1865,
Company K:			
First Lieutenant....	Luman M. White........	....	June 8, 1865,
Second Lieutenant..	Henry C. Burke.........	Philadelphia.....	June 8, 1865,

OFFICERS OF THE 200th REGIMENT, INFANTRY.

RANK.	NAME.	CO. OF RESIDENCE.	DATE OF RANK.	REMARKS.
Quartermaster.......	Benjamin F. Eberly......	Cumberland......	April 14, 1865,	....
Company A:				
Captain...............	John Wimer...............	York...............	Feb. 3, 1865,	....
First Lieutenant....	Edward Smith.............	Do................	Feb. 3, 1865,	....
Second Lieutenant.	Jeremiah Oliver..........	Do................	Feb. 3, 1865,	....
Company B:				
Captain...............	Abraham R. Royer......	Berks...............	Mar. 31, 1865,	....
First Lieutenant....	John S. Mackinson......	Dauphin...........	Mar. 31, 1865,	....
Company C:				
Second Lieutenant.	George S. Marrett.......	Cumberland......	Mar. 14, 1865,	....
Company K:				
First Lieutenant....	Augustus C. Stieg.......	York...............	Jan. 21, 1865,	....

EXECUTIVE MILITARY DEPARTMENT.

RANK.	NAME.	CO. OF RESIDENCE.	DATE OF RANK.	REMARKS.
Company E:				
Second Lieutenant.	William M. Kinzer	Luzerne	Nov. 13, 1864,	
Company I:				
Captain	Alexander M'Cormick	Dauphin	Jan. 28, 1865,	
First Lieutenant	Stephen O. M'Curdy	Franklin	Jan. 28, 1865,	
Second Lieutenant	Abner Bingaman	Dauphin	Jan. 28, 1865,	

OFFICERS OF THE 202d REGIMENT, INFANTRY.

RANK.	NAME.	CO. OF RESIDENCE.	DATE OF RANK.	REMARKS.
Company E:				
Second Lieutenant.	Alfred Mellin	Lehigh	April 5, 1865,	
Company H:				
Captain	Josiah B. Cobaugh	Cumberland	Nov. 13, 1864,	
First Lieutenant	Samuel Byer	Do	Nov. 13, 1864,	
Second Lieutenant	John Milton Hays	Do	April 17, 1865,	

OFFICERS OF THE 203d REGIMENT, INFANTRY.

RANK.	NAME.	CO. OF RESIDENCE.	DATE OF RANK.	REMARKS.
Colonel	Oliver P. Harding	Luzerne	Jan. 16, 1865,	Dismissed the service
Do	Amos W. Bachman	Lancaster	May 3, 1865,	
Lieutenant Colonel	Amos W. Bachman	Do	Jan. 16, 1865,	To Colonel
Do	Benjamin Brooke	Delaware	May 3, 1865,	
Major	Michael J. Cooke	Philadelphia	Jan. 16, 1865,	
Company A:				
Captain	George W. Mason	Lancaster	Jan. 16, 1865,	
First Lieutenant	William R. G. Boggs	Chester	Jan. 16, 1865,	
Second Lieutenant	Ephraim Potts	Lancaster	Jan. 16, 1865,	
Company C:				
Captain	Charles B. Duncan	Philadelphia	Jan. 16, 1865,	
Company D:				
Second Lieutenant	John Lee	Philadelphia	Jan. 16, 1865,	
Company E:				
First Lieutenant	Johnson Hubbell	Philadelphia	Jan. 16, 1865,	
Second Lieutenant	Michael K. Minich	Do	Jan. 16, 1865,	
Company F:				
Captain	James Mulherin	Philadelphia	Jan. 16, 1865,	
First Lieutenant	Robert Anderson	Do	Jan. 16, 1865,	
Second Lieutenant	Monroe J. Horner	Do	Jan. 16, 1865,	

Company G :			
First Lieutenant	De Forest F. Wheeler...	Lycoming........	Dec. 30, 1864,
Company H :			
First Lieutenant.....	Richard W. Hemphill..	Philadelphia.....	Jan. 16, 1865,
Do....	John S. Wetter.........	....Do...........	May 26, 1865,
Second Lieutenant. .	Benjamin F. Landis....	Lancaster	Jan. 16, 1865,
Company I :			
Second Lieutenant. .	William D. Geise.......	Lycoming	April 29, 1865,
Company K :			
Second Lieutenant. .	Joseph K. Potts.........	Lancaster	May 26, 1865,

OFFICERS THE OF 204th REGIMEMT, FIFTH ARTILLERY.

RANK.	NAME.	CO. OF RESIDENCE.	DATE OF RANK.	REMARKS.
Major	William H. Hope	Allegheny	Mar. 25, 1865,	
Company A :				
Captain	Albert Peart	Allegheny	Mar. 25, 1865,	
First Lieutenant	Robert Alexander	Do	Mar. 25, 1865,	
Second Lieutenant	Jesse Hildebrand	Do	Mar. 25, 1865,	
Do	Frederick Metzger	Do	Mar. 25, 1865,	
Company C :				
First Lieutenant	Carrol A. M'Gaw	Allegheny	Mar. 25, 1865,	
Second Lieutenant	Wm. J. Donahue	Do	Mar. 25, 1865,	
Company H :				
Captain	George W. Smith	Allegheny	Mar. 25, 1865,	

EXECUTIVE MILITARY DEPARTMENT. 221

OFFICERS OF THE 205th REGIMENT, INFANTRY.

RANK.	NAME.	CO. OF RESIDENCE.	DATE OF RANK.	REMARKS.
Company C:				
First Lieutenant...	David M. Butler.........	Blair.............	April 3, 1865,	....
Second Lieutenant.	John H. Robertson......	Do.............	April 3, 1865,	....
Company G:				
Captain............	Ambrose M. Aults......	Blair.............	Dec. 23, 1864,	....
First Lieutenant...	Robert A. Sharp........	Franklin.........	Dec. 23, 1864,	....
Second Lieutenant.	George W. Clymens....	Fulton...........	Dec. 23, 1864,	....
Company H:				
First Lieutenant...	George W. White.......	Lancaster........	April 3, 1865,	....
Second Lieutenant.	Irwin S. Phillips.........	Berks............	April 3, 1865,	....
Company I:				
Captain............	John A. M'Cahen......	Blair.............	Oct. 30, 1864,	....
First Lieutenant...	Henry Hawk............	Do.............	Oct. 30, 1864,	....

OFFICERS OF THE 206th REGIMENT, INFANTRY.

RANK.	NAME.	CO. OF RESIDENCE.	DATE OF RANK.	REMARKS.
Company I:				
Second Lieutenant.	Samuel I. Conrad.......	Indiana..........	Jan. 19, 1865,	....

OFFICERS OF THE 207th REGIMENT, INFANTRY.

BANK.	NAME.	CO. OF RESIDENCE.	DATE OF RANK.	REMARKS.
Company B:				
First Lieutenant....	Jacob E. Schambacher..	Tioga............	April 3, 1865,	....
Second Lieutenant..	T. S. Knapp..............	Bradford........	April 3, 1865,	....
Company F:				
First Lieutenant....	David L. Powders......	Franklin.........	Feb. 6, 1865,	....
Company H:				
First Lieutenant....	Amasa Culver...........	Tioga.............	May 24, 1865,	....
Second Lieutenant..	Oliver P. Babcock......	....Do............	May 24, 1865,	....
Company I:				
Captain...............	Charles A. Brion........	Lycoming......	April 3, 1865,	....
First Lieutenant....	James E. Fry.............	......Do...........	April 3, 1865,	....
Second Lieutenant..	Wm. B. Caselberry....	......Do...........	April 3, 1865,	....
Company K:				
Second Lieutenant..	William L. Rees.........	Tioga.............	April 3, 1865,	....

EXECUTIVE MILITARY DEPARTMENT. 223

OFFICERS OF THE 208th REGIMENT, INFANTRY.

RANK.	NAME.	CO. OF RESIDENCE.	DATE OF RANK.	REMARKS.
Company C:				
Captain	William C. I. Smith	Lebanon	June 3, 1865	
First Lieutenant	Alfred Corl	Do	June 3, 1865	
Second Lieutenant	William H. Bordner	Do	June 3, 1865	
Company D:				
First Lieutenant	Wm. H. Gemberling	Snyder	Mar. 26, 1865	
Second Lieutenant	Charles B. Miller	Do	Mar. 26, 1865	

OFFICERS OF THE 209th REGIMENT, INFANTRY.

RANK.	NAME.	CO. OF RESIDENCE.	DATE OF RANK.	REMARKS.
Company B:				
Second Lieutenant..	Wm. B. Morrow	York	Mar. 24, 1865,	
Company C:				
Second Lieutenant..	Samuel Singleton	Cambria	Mar. 28, 1865,	
Company D:				
Captain	Noah W. Kuhn	Franklin	April 3, 1865,	
First Lieutenant	Benjamin F. Deal	Do	April 3, 1865,	
Second Lieutenant..	George J. Dietrich	Do	April 3, 1865,	
Company F:				
Captain	Henry A. Bigler	Lancaster	May 16, 1865,	
First Lieutenant	Lazarus Minich	Cumberland	May 16, 1865,	
Second Lieutenant..	Samuel B. Smith	Perry	May 16, 1865,	
Company G:				
First Lieutenant	Calvin R. Snyder	Adams	Dec. 20, 1864,	
Second Lieutenant..	J. Howard Wert	Do	Dec. 20, 1864,	
Company H:				
Captain	William Kerr	Lehigh	Mar. 29, 1865,	
First Lieutenant	Lewis Fink	Do	Mar. 29, 1865,	
Second Lieutenant..	David B. Overholt	Do	Mar. 29, 1865,	

EXECUTIVE MILITARY DEPARTMENT. 225

OFFICERS OF THE 210th REGIMENT, INFANTRY.

RANK.	NAME.	CO. OF RESIDENCE.	DATE OF RANK.	REMARKS.
Major	James H. Graves	Potter	Nov. 26, 1864,	
Adjutant	Morris Schlesinger		Dec. 27, 1864,	
Quartermaster	Joseph A. Clark	Montour	Feb. 14, 1865,	
Company B:				
Captain	John W. Hughes		Dec. 8, 1864,	
First Lieutenant	William H. Evans	Columbia	Dec. 8, 1864,	
Company D:				
Second Lieutenant	E. W. Meisenhelder		Feb. 3, 1865,	
Company F:				
Captain	Alanson T. Kinney	Potter	Nov. 26, 1864,	
First Lieutenant	George F. Rowlee	Do	Nov. 26, 1864,	
Second Lieutenant	William M. Colwell	Do	Nov. 26, 1864,	
Company I:				
Captain	James A. Foster	Bradford	Jan. 17, 1865,	
First Lieutenant	John C. Martin		Jan. 17, 1865,	

15 Military Depart.

OFFICERS OF THE 211th REGIMENT, INFANTRY.

RANK.	NAME.	CO. OF RESIDENCE.	DATE OF RANK.	REMARKS.
Colonel.............	Levi A. Dodd...........	Westmoreland...	Mar. 19, 1865,	....
Lieutenant Colonel..	Augustus A. Mechling.	....Do............	Mar. 19, 1865,	Resigned ....
Do.............	William A. Coulter.....	Mercer...........	April 12, 1865,	....
Major.............	H. King Smith.........	Allegheny........	April 12, 1865,	....
Adjutant.............	Herman F. Steck........	Jefferson.........	April 12, 1865,	....
Company A:				
Second Lieutenant..	Henry A. Bagley.......	Crawford.........	April 12, 1865,	....
Company B:				
Captain.............	Charles J. Wilson.......	Jefferson.........	April 12, 1865,	....
First Lieutenant.....	Milion H. M'Anineh....	....Do............	April 12, 1865,	....
Company C:				
First Lieutenant.....	John M. Pelton.........	M'Kean...........	April 12, 1865,	....
Do.............	William C. Smith.......	Jefferson.........	May 28, 1865,	....
Second Lieutenant..	William C. Smith.......	....Do............	April 12, 1865,	To First Lieutenant......
Do.............	Horace H. Sparks.......	....Do............	May 28, 1865,	....
Company D:				
Captain.............	Thomas C. Gibson......	Mercer...........	April 12, 1865,	....
First Lieutenant.....	James F. Johnston......	....Do............	April 13, 1865,	....
Second Lieutenant..	James F. Johnston......	....Do............	April 12, 1865,	To First Lieutenant......
Do.............	William R. Moore......	....Do............	April 13, 1865,	....
Company E:				
First Lieutenant.....	Lewis Thompson........	Westmoreland...	Feb. 3, 1865,	....

Company H:				
Second Lieutenant..	Joseph S. M'Quaide....	Westmoreland...	Jan. 21, 1865,	
Company K:				
First Lieutenant....	William B. Chain......	Westmoreland...	April 12, 1865,	
Second Lieutenant..	William B. Chain......	......Do	Nov. 6, 1864,	To First Lieutenant......

OFFICERS OF THE 212th REGIMENT, SIXTH ARTILLERY.

RANK.	NAME.	CO. OF RESIDENCE.	DATE OF RANK.	REMARKS.
Company A:				
Captain............	William R. Hutchison..	Butler.........	Sept. 10, 1864,	
First Lieutenant....	Thomas H. M'Ilvaine....	Do.........	Sept. 13, 1864,	
Do............	H. W. M'Candless.	Do.........	Sept. 13, 1864,	
Second Lieutenant..	James Harvey...........	Do.........	Nov. 1, 1864,	
Do............	Milton Wolford	Do.........	Nov. 1, 1864,	
Company B:				
Captain............	Gustavus L. Braun......	Allegheny......	Sept. 10, 1864,	
First Lieutenant....	W. H. H. Wassen	Butler.........	Sept. 14, 1864,	
Do............	John M. Kelsey	Allegheny......	Sept. 14, 1864,	
Second Lieutenant..	Robert O Shira.........	Butler.........	Nov. 1, 1864,	
Do............	William C. Rudyard....	Allegheny......	Nov. 1, 1864,	
Company C:				
Captain............	David Evans...	Allegheny......	Sept. 10, 1864,	
First Lieutenant....	William Rowden........	Do	Sept. 10, 1864,	
Do............	Joseph J. Grubbs...... .	Do	Sept. 10, 1864,	
Second Lieutenant..	Thomas E. Sturgeon.....	Do	Nov. 1, 1864,	
Do............	George Sneed...........	Do	Nov. 1, 1864,	
Company D:				
Captain............	Daniel Gravatte.........	Allegheny......	Sept. 13, 1864,	
First Lieutenant....	James K. Irwin.........	Westmoreland ...	Sept. 13, 1864,	
Do............	John C. Anderson.......	Allegheny......	Sept. 13, 1864,	
Second Lieutenant..	James G. Stewart.......	Westmoreland ...	Nov. 1, 1864,	
Do............	William W. Hill.........	Allegheny......	Nov. 1, 1864,	

EXECUTIVE MILITARY DEPARTMENT. 229

Company E :			
Captain	Joseph Keepers	Fayette	Sept. 13, 1864,
First Lieutenant	Samuel A. Barr	Allegheny	Sept. 13, 1864,
Do	Thomas M. Fee	Fayette	Sept. 13, 1864,
Second Lieutenant	James W. Downer	Washington	Nov. 1, 1864,
Do	Martin O. Lane	Allegheny	Nov. 1, 1864,
Company F :			
Captain	William H. Obey	Allegheny	Sept. 12, 1864,
First Lieutenant	Thomas Welsh	Do	Sept. 12, 1864,
Do	John M. Larimer	Do	Sept. 15, 1864,
Second Lieutenant	William C. Barnett	Do	Nov. 1, 1864,
Do	Frederick Ruch	Do	Nov. 1, 1864,
Company G :			
Captain	Charles F. Hadley	Allegheny	Sept. 15, 1864,
First Lieutenant	Alfred W. Kredel	Do	Sept. 15, 1864,
Do	John A. Irwin	Do	Sept. 15, 1864,
Second Lieutenant	John Hoedle	Do	Nov. 1, 1864,
Do	William C. Brown	Do	Nov. 1, 1864,
Company H :			
Captain	Malachi Leslie	Westmoreland	Sept. 10, 1864,
First Lieutenant	Charles S. Miller	Allegheny	Sept. 10, 1864,
Do	William H. Drury	Do	Sept. 10, 1864,
Second Lieutenant	Joseph Cline	Armstrong	Nov. 1, 1864,
Do	Robert Machisney	Allegheny	Nov. 1, 1864,
Company I :			
Captain	Wm. H. M'Candless	Lawrence	Sept. 8, 1864,
First Lieutenant	Robert E. Barnett	Do	Sept. 8, 1864,
Do	William J. Kirker	Do	Sept. 8, 1864,

TWO HUNDRED AND TWELFTH REGIMENT—Continued.

RANK.	NAME.	CO. OF RESIDENCE.	DATE OF RANK.	REMARKS.
Second Lieutenant.	James M. Miller	Lawrence	Nov. 1, 1864,	
Do	David W. Aken	Do	Nov. 1, 1864,	
Company K:				
Captain	Thomas A. Stone	Fayette	Sept. 13, 1864,	
First Lieutenant	John Bierer	Do	Sept. 13, 1864,	
Do	Lucius S. Bunting	Do	Sept. 15, 1864,	
Second Lieutenant.	Henry White	Do	Nov. 1, 1864,	
Do	Andrew J. Dean	Do	Dec. 29, 1864,	
Company L:				
Captain	David Cornelius	Allegheny	Sept. 12, 1864,	
First Lieutenant	Henry M'Ormick	Westmoreland	Sept. 12, 1864,	
Do	William W. Kennedy	Allegheny	Sept. 12, 1864,	
Second Lieutenant.	William T. Black	Do	Nov. 1, 1864,	
Do	William Winebrenner	Westmoreland	Nov. 1, 1864,	
Company M:				
Captain	Cornelius J. Watson	Lawrence	Sept. 13, 1864,	
First Lieutenant	George D. Brown	Do	Sept. 13, 1864,	
Do	Marinus K. M'Dowell	Do	Sept. 13, 1864,	
Second Lieutenant.	Joseph Hunter	Do	Nov. 1, 1864,	
Do	Marcus C. Rose	Mercer	Nov. 1, 1864,	

EXECUTIVE MILITARY DEPARTMENT. 231

OFFICERS OF THE 213th REGIMENT, INFANTRY.

RANK.	NAME.	CO. OF RESIDENCE.	DATE OF RANK.	REMARKS.
Colonel............	John A. Gorgas............	Philadelphia......	Mar. 7, 1865,	....
Lieutenant Colonel.	Jacob M. Davis............	....Do	Mar. 7, 1865,	....
Major................	Enos R. Artman............	Bucks	Mar. 20, 1865,	....
Adjutant............	James L. M'Ilhenny.......	Philadelphia......	Mar. 7, 1865,	....
Quartermaster......	Francis A. Chadwick.......	....Do	Mar. 7, 1865,	....
Company A :				
Captain............	W. H. M'Minn.............	Philadelphia......	Mar. 5, 1865,	....
First Lieutenant...	Charles W. Bender.........	....Do	Mar. 5, 1865,	....
Second Lieutenant.	James M. Anthony.........	....Do	Mar. 20, 1865,	....
Company B :				
Captain............	James N. Blundin.........	Philadelphia......	Mar. 5, 1865,	....
First Lieutenant...	Frank D. Bingham........	....Do	Mar. 5, 1865,	....
Second Lieutenant.	Borodail Browne...........	....Do	Mar. 5, 1865,	....
Company C :				
Captain............	S. W. Pettit..............	Philadelphia......	Mar. 5, 1865,	....
First Lieutenant...	James Davis...............	....Do	Mar. 7, 1865,	....
Second Lieutenant.	H. S. Godshall............	....Do	Mar. 5, 1865,	....
Company D :				
Captain............	John Kennedy.............	Berks............	Mar. 8, 1865,	....
First Lieutenant...	Lemuel Buch.............	....Do	Mar. 8, 1865,	....
Second Lieutenant.	Allison Leininger.........	....Do	Mar. 8, 1865,	Resigned.........
Do	Robert N. Barber.........	Philadelphia......	May 30, 1865,	....

… ANNUAL REPORT OF THE

TWO HUNDRED AND THIRTEENTH REGIMENT—Continued.

RANK.	NAME.	CO. OF RESIDENCE.	DATE OF RANK.	REMARKS.
Company E:				
Captain............	Henry C. Williams......	Philadelphia.....	Mar. 7, 1865,	....
First Lieutenant....	Francis Randolph	Do	Mar. 7, 1865,	....
Second Lieutenant..	Walter S. Dowell	Chester..........	Mar. 7, 1865,	....
Company F:				
Captain............	Richard W. Davis.......	Philadelphia.....	Mar. 20, 1865,	....
First Lieutenant....	Thomas M. Bender......	Do	Mar. 7, 1865,	....
Second Lieutenant..	Horace M. Rowand.....	Do..........	Mar. 20, 1865,	....
Company G:				
Captain............	William Babe...........	Philadelphia.....	Mar. 5, 1865,	....
First Lieutenant....	Martin L Littlefield	Juniata	Mar. 5, 1865,	....
Second Lieutenant..	James Carrick	Delaware.........	Mar. 5, 1865,	....
Company H:				
Captain............	Theodore A. Snyder....	Philadelphia.....	Mar. 6, 1865,	....
First Lieutenant....	John Smith.............	Do	Mar. 6, 1865,	....
Second Lieutenant..	George C. Henszey......	Do	Mar. 20, 1865,	....
Company I:				
Captain............	Enos R. Artman........	Bucks............	Mar. 6, 1865,	To Major.
Do................	Cephas W. Dyer........	Do	Mar. 20, 1865,	....
First Lieutenant....	Cephas W. Dyer........	Do	Mar. 6, 1865,	To Captain......
Do................	Samuel F. Ball..........	Philadelphia.....	Mar. 20, 1865,	....

Second Lieutenant..	Samuel F. Ball............	Philadelphia......	Mar. 6, 1865,	To First Lieutenant.
Do.............	Christopher Wyckoff....	......Do..............	Mar. 20, 1865,	
Company K:				
Captain...............	Lewis Stanton............	Philadelphia......	Mar. 7, 1865,	
First Lieutenant.....	Frederick L. Mannes...	...... Do.............	Mar. 7, 1865,	
Second Lieutenant .	Jacob Churchill.........	......Do.............	Mar. 7, 1865,	

OFFICERS OF THE 214th REGIMENT, INFANTRY.

RANK.	NAME.	CO. OF RESIDENCE.	DATE OF RANK.	REMARKS.
Colonel	David B. M'Kibbin	Philadelphia	April 5, 1865	
Lieutenant Colonel	W. H. Harrison	Do	April 7, 1865	
Major	W. M. Worrall	Do	April 3, 1865	
Adjutant	Wm. M. Buddy	Do	April 3, 1865	
Quartermaster	C. H. Fernald	Do	Mar. 20, 1865	
Company A:				
Captain	Charles D. Foy	Philadelphia	Mar. 24, 1865	
First Lieutenant	Henry H. Badger	Do	Mar. 24, 1865	To Captain Company F.
Second Lieutenant	John H. Frederick	Do	Mar. 24, 1865	
Company B:				
Captain	James L. Benson	Lancaster	April 7, 1865	
First Lieutenant	Jacob R. Witmer	Do	April 7, 1865	
Second Lieutenant	Michael Kreiner	Do	April 7, 1865	Discharged
Do	Edward Kempfle	Do	July 19, 1865	
Company C:				
Captain	John F. Snyder	Philadelphia	April 2, 1865	
First Lieutenant	Walter Eckel	Do	April 2, 1865	
Second Lieutenant	W. Morris Cox	Do	April 2, 1865	
Company D:				
Captain	Thomas S. Mason	Philadelphia	April 3, 1865	
First Lieutenant	James C. Linton	Do	April 3, 1865	
Second Lieutenant	Thomas C. Stokes	Do	April 3, 1865	

EXECUTIVE MILITARY DEPARTMENT. 235

Company E:				
Captain..........	David Richardson, Jr..	Philadelphia......	April 1, 1865,	
First Lieutenant....	E. M. Croll.............	Do	April 1, 1865,	
Second Lieutenant..	Wm. A. V. Porter.......	Do	April 3, 1865,	
Company F:				
Captain..........	Thomas F. Coryell......	Philadelphia......	April 7, 1865,	Dismissed............
Do	Henry H. Badger........	Do	Oct. 1, 1865,	
First Lieutenant....	Presley C. Chaplin......	Do	April 7, 1865,	
Second Lieutenant..	George D. Coleman......	Do	April 7, 1865,	
Company G:				
Captain..........	Robert H. Ford.........	Philadelphia......	April 3, 1865,	
First Lieutenant....	Estell E. Gilbert........	Do	April 3, 1865,	
Second Lieutenant..	James B. Graham.......	Do	April 3, 1865,	
Company H:				
Captain..........	Edward Kelley..........	Northampton.....	April 2, 1865,	
First Lieutenant....	Henry L. Arndt.........	Do	April 2, 1865,	
Second Lieutenant..	Joseph S. Osterstoak....	Do	April 2, 1865,	
Company I:				
Captain..........	Mark Walker............	Philadelphia......	April 2, 1865,	
First Lieutenant....	Joseph F. Sweeton......	Do	April 2, 1865,	
Second Lieutenant..	Thomas Corley.........	Do	April 2, 1865,	
Company K:				
Captain..........	Thomas Ford............	Philadelphia......	Mar. 27, 1865,	
First Lieutenant....	Edward E. Burr.........	Do	Mar. 27, 1865,	Discharged...........
Do	R. Frank Walborn.......	Do	July 12, 1865,	
Second Lieutenant..	R. Frank Walborn.......	Do	Mar. 27, 1865,	
Do	Theodore Gilbert.......	Do	July 12, 1865,	To First Lieutenant.

OFFICERS OF THE 215th REGIMENT, INFANTRY.

RANK.	NAME.	CO. OF RESIDENCE.	DATE OF RANK.	REMARKS.
Colonel	Francis Wister	Philadelphia	April 21, 1865	
Lieutenant Colonel	Francis B. Jones	Do	April 16, 1865	
Major	Andrew T. Goodman	Do	April 21, 1865	
Adjutant	Thomas C. Rea	Do	April 18, 1865	
Quartermaster	Joseph S. Gillespie	Do	April 26, 1865	
Company A:				
Captain	John W. Ryan	Philadelphia	April 11, 1865	
First Lieutenant	Alexander Skilton	Do	April 11, 1865	
Second Lieutenant	Joseph J. Fitzgerald	Do	April 11, 1865	
Company B:				
Captain	George H. Ettla	Lancaster	April 18, 1865	
First Lieutenant	Nelson Haas	Do	April 16, 1865	
Second Lieutenant	Abraham B. Cassel	Do	April 18, 1865	
Company C:				
Captain	Timothy Cadwallader	Bucks	April 13, 1865	
First Lieutenant	Nahum K. Richardson	Philadelphia	April 13, 1865	
Second Lieutenant	John F. Jerme	Do	April 25, 1865	
Company D:				
Captain	Richard O. Wilson	Philadelphia	April 13, 1865	
First Lieutenant	Theodore O. Rose	Do	April 13, 1865	
Second Lieutenant	Michael O. Morgan	Do	April 13, 1865	

EXECUTIVE MILITARY DEPARTMENT. 237

Company E:			
Captain	William J. Wallace	Philadelphia	April 25, 1865,
First Lieutenant	Wm. H. Duckstien	Do	April 13, 1865,
Second Lieutenant	Francis Bregy, Jr	Do	April 13, 1865,
Company F:			
Captain	James V. Schreiner	Philadelphia	April 18, 1865,
First Lieutenant	Caspar Cooper	Do	April 18, 1865,
Second Lieutenant	Andrew J. M'Lardy	Do	April 18, 1865,
Company G:			
Captain	John O. Bilheimer	Northampton	April 18, 1865,
First Lieutenant	John F. Kress	Do	April 18, 1865,
Second Lieutenant	Augustus Stewart	Do	April 18, 1865,
Company H:			
Captain	Andrew Deibley	Lancaster	April 21, 1865,
First Lieutenant	E. Schaeffer Metzger	Do	April 21, 1865,
Second Lieutenant	John R. Garden	Do	April 21, 1865,
Company I:			
Captain	William Rush	Philadelphia	April 13, 1865,
First Lieutenant	John W. Crothers	Do	April 13, 1865,
Second Lieutenant	Henry E. Wilkinson	Do	April 13, 1865,
Company K:			
Captain	Alexander Gray	Philadelphia	April 15, 1865,
First Lieutenant	Samuel C. Stretch	Do	April 15, 1865,
Second Lieutenant	Samuel L. Ely	Bucks	April 26, 1865,

OFFICERS OF THE WARREN COUNTY RIFLES.

RANK.	NAME.	CO. OF RESIDENCE.	DATE OF RANK.	REMARKS.
Captain.............	Sylvester H. Davis......	Warren...............	Mar. 1, 1865,	....
First Lieutenant.....	George W. M'Pherson....	....Do................	Mar. 1, 1865,	....
Second Lieutenant...	Amos E. Goodrich.......	....Do................	Mar. 1, 1865,	....

OFFICERS OF INDEPENDENT BATTERY C.

RANK.	NAME.	CO. OF RESIDENCE.	DATE OF RANK.	REMARKS.
First Lieutenant.....	James Mitchell...........	Allegheny..........	Feb. 8, 1865,	....
Second Lieutenant...	William H. Bruce........	Beaver.............	Feb. 8, 1865,	....

OFFICERS OF INDEPENDENT BATTERY F.

RANK.	NAME.	CO. OF RESIDENCE.	DATE OF RANK.	REMARKS.
First Lieutenant	Samuel D. Glass	Allegheny	Jan. 4, 1865,	Term expired.
Do	Frederick L. Atwood	Do	Feb. 19, 1865,	
Do	George Ritchie	Do	Feb. 24, 1865,	
Second Lieutenant	George Ritchie	Do	Jan. 4, 1865,	To First Lieutenant
Do	Frank H. Shiras	Do	Feb. 19, 1865,	
Do	Frank A. Merrick	Beaver	Feb. 24, 1865,	

OFFICERS OF INDEPENDENT BATTERY H.

RANK.	NAME.	CO. OF RESIDENCE.	DATE OF RANK.	REMARKS.
Captain	Edwin H. Nevins, Jr	Allegheny	Mar. 8, 1865,	
First Lieutenant	Wm. H. Askine	Do	Mar. 8, 1865,	
Second Lieutenant	Wm. F. Hoag	Do	Mar. 8, 1865,	

EXECUTIVE OFFICE, MILITARY DEPARTMENT,
Harrisburg, December 1, 1865.

R. BIDDLE ROBERTS, *Col. and A. D. C.*
SAMUEL B. THOMAS, *Col. and A. D. C.*

Printed in Dunstable, United Kingdom